Redemption Has 4 Paws

How all the dogs in my life helped me find
my life's purpose and redeem myself

Robin Kashuba

ISBN 978-1-64003-210-1 (Paperback)
ISBN 978-1-64003-211-8 (Digital)

Library of Congress Control Number: 2017953237

Covenant Books, Inc.
11661 Hwy 707
Murrells Inlet, SC 29576
www.covenantbooks.com

ACKNOWLEDGMENTS

I have so many people that I want to thank that inspired me or supported me on my journey writing this book. Where do I start? I'll start with my parents. My mom gave both my sister and I our love of reading. And because of that love of reading, by extension she encouraged me in writing. My father gave me my love of animals, and in particular, dogs. I'm so thankful that dad relented and brought Tammy, our first sheltie, into my life.

Thanks to my sister, Linda, for her continual encouragement. Thanks to my friend Kit who read the first draft of the book and gave me ideas to improve the book.

Thanks to all my friends who read a draft of the book and gave me their critique and suggestions to make the book better. I took all of your comments to heart and made changes where necessary.

I would also like to thank all those who contributed to my GoFundMe page to get this book published. I don't want to list you out separately as my GoFundMe campaign is still going on as I write this page. But you know who you are whether you put your credit card number onto the page or sent me checks or sent cash. Your faith in me and this book literally brought me to tears and I am forever grateful to you for your faith and help.

Thanks to all the dogs in my life: Dogs that have given me unconditional love and a wealth of stories to tell. While writing this book I was transported back in time, and remembering some of these fur angels and their antics brought me to tears and laughter. These 4-legged "furkids" have had such a big influence on me and I'm forever grateful that every one of them has had a part in my life story.

Thanks to all the members of my therapy dog group. Making visits with you has been such a bright spot in my life. It gives me such joy to see how people we visit react so positively to the various dogs that come and visit them. You are all volunteers and the fact that you faithfully take your personal time to brighten other's lives says a lot about what wonderful people you all are. Thanks for making visits with me!

A huge thank you to all the rescues out there who do difficult work trying to find homes for the dogs in their care. I have fostered, transported and adopted dogs from several rescues in my area. I can't say enough about the wonderful work that they do. In particular, I would like to thank the following rescues who have let me adopt some of my best friends and companions: Minnesota Wisconsin Collie Rescue, Minnesota Sheltie Rescue, Long Island Shetland Sheepdog Rescue and Central Illinois Sheltie Rescue. I love every one of the dogs that you have allowed me to adopt whether they became therapy dogs or not. Thank you!

Thanks to every friend and even the foes in my life. Each of you has helped me become the person I am. Even the negative events that I have weathered in my life have spurred me to make positive changes in my life.

I want to thank my ex-husband Glen for being willing to read my book and give me his critique, memories and pictures to be used in the book. While you and I did not take enough care to keep our marriage alive and well, we did share the love of all the dogs that have spent time in our lives. I'm grateful for all the love and care you have given to each of our "furkids".

I want to express my most humble apologies to "Tom". You were so willing to give me your love at a time that I needed it and you were patient to stand by me for so many years. I am deeply sorry that I hurt you—that was not my intention at all. I do hope you have found joy, love and happiness in your life.

My biggest and deepest thanks go to God. Thank you for the life you have given me. While I have failed to live up to your laws and commandments, I know that you have forgiven me for the many mistakes, hurts and lies I have perpetrated on other people. I am trying my best every day to live a more honest, more giving and more loving life. I have a long way to go but with your love, I can only move forward to help other people and animals. Thanks so much for this life you have let me lead!

INTRODUCTION

Dogs, as they say, are man's best friend. Well, actually, they are woman's best friend too. Some of my best friends and closest confidants have four legs and tails. It seems that dogs have captivated the human race with their silly puppy antics, their unconditional love, and by how well they work with and for us. Dogs have performed a myriad of duties for people by herding sheep and cattle, by sniffing bombs at airports or in war zones, by guarding property and homes, by serving people with disabilities, and by just lending an ear to their owner without conditions, advice, or negative remarks.

This book is the odyssey of my life and how every dog that has been a part of my life has helped me through some of the toughest times I have had to face, but better than that, they have brought me to find my true life's purpose. Every one of these faithful companions has been a treasured friend to me. They have been there for me through thick and thin, good times and bad, and asked nothing more from me than to feed them twice a day, let them out to go to the bathroom and give them a soft stroke on their fur.

While this book is about all the dogs I've loved throughout my life, it's also a book about therapy dogs and how I deeply treasure each and every one of my therapy dogs—registered or not. Several of my dogs are rescues, several I purchased from breeders, but all of them have entered my home with a willingness to be a partner to me in whatever I ask of them. I don't ever get any lip or back talk from them.

My goal in writing this book is 5-fold:

First, I want to get down on paper all the dogs that have spent time in my world, how each of them has affected me in so many positive ways and to let the reader have a laugh over some of the she-nanigans that some of my dogs have played.

Second, I want the reader to understand how important dog rescues are in finding good homes for unwanted animals. But I also want the reader to know that there are good breeders out there and if you have your heart set on a particular breed and want a puppy, then do your homework and find out all you can about the breeder and your chosen breed.

Third, I want to be an advocate for deaf dogs. Many deaf dogs were and still are put down on a daily basis because they aren't "perfect". There are some breeders who will breed 2 dogs together that shouldn't be bred at all just for the sake of getting a show ring champion. I have 3 deaf dogs—dogs bred by crossing two blue merles or a blue merle with a dog that has the merle gene— in my pack and I have found they are more attentive and more loving than my hearing dogs. Maybe I got lucky or maybe deaf dogs truly are special.

Fourth, I would love to see every dog owner that has a dog that would make a good therapy dog prospect take classes and pass a therapy dog exam. Then get out there and start making visits. You will be amazed at how much more you get out of making therapy visits with your dog as well as the people you are visiting. There is no better feeling than putting a smile on the face of a lonely elderly person in a nursing home or seeing a child become comfortable reading to your dog and starting to comprehend what they are reading. Believe me, you get so much more back in spades than you give.

Fifth, I want to tell you the story of my three deaf shelties—Skylar, Olaf and MacPherson. Skylar was the first deaf dog to enter my life and she taught me so much about patience and how our 4-legged friends live life to the fullest despite a disability. Olaf is my second deaf Sheltie and truly a "devil in a dog suit". This fun-loving dog led me to solidify my life's purpose of making visits to people with my therapy dogs despite all the naughty and devilish things he has done while in my household. Even though he is boisterous, steals food off my counters at any opportunity, chews up paper, books and magazines by the dozen, he has a heart of gold and wants to love everyone. And finally there is MacPherson or Mackie P as I call him.

This dog is a true example of how life should be lived—he loves everyone and every animal and only wants to please the people in his life. He is truly inspirational as far as living a good and loving life despite whatever shortcomings may come our way.

So settle down with a glass of wine or a cup of coffee and take the journey of my life along with me and my dogs. See you at the end.

CHAPTER ONE

The Devil Went Down to Minnesota

By January of 2015, winter was dragging on in Minnesota. Cold and snow had visited us and stayed since early November 2014, and the winter seemed to be never ending. One particularly cold evening at the end of January, I was spending time on Facebook when a posting from the Long Island Shetland Sheepdog Rescue appeared in my newsfeed. The picture was of a beautiful blue merle sheltie with an abundance of white in his coat. He had two bright blue eyes and, according to the post, a personality that won him many friends. His only issue was that he was deaf. I contacted the rescue and asked if they adopted outside the New York area. They asked me to fill out their application online and would get back to me.

I had already adopted two shelties from rescues and had purchased a deaf sheltie the year before, so I was up for adopting another deaf dog—especially if I could use him for therapy work. I filled out the application and gave references of the Minnesota Sheltie Rescue and the Minnesota Wisconsin Collie Rescue—two rescues from which I had previously fostered and adopted dogs. The LISSR got back to me right away, saying that I was the kind of adopter they were hoping would adopt Olaf. They asked me if I did indeed want to adopt him. I told them I was very interested in adopting him but that I couldn't afford to fly him from New York to Minnesota. That's no problem, they told me.

Within a week, they had formed a transportation plan to get Olaf from New York to Eau Claire, Wisconsin, where I would pick him up and bring him back to Minnesota. I had called on a couple of friends of mine in the collie rescue to help drive him from Milwaukee to Eau Claire.

So bright and early on the morning of February 7, Olaf made the trek from Pennsylvania, where his foster mom had driven him the night before, all the way to Eau Claire, where I picked him up at seven forty-five in the evening.

I hadn't slept at all the night before. I was so excited to add this beautiful creature to my pack, but I was also conflicted about adding yet another dog to my pack. I tossed and turned all night, and I'm sure my lack of sleep made me look like a character from a horror movie as I set off in my car on my newest adventure with dogs.

A couple of my friends from the collie rescue rode with me. We stopped for late lunch, early dinner in Hudson, Wisconsin. It was fairly obvious to my friends that I was literally aglow with excitement at adding Olaf into my pack. Yet I was still wavering back and forth in my mind on whether it was right to add another dog to my pack. But my ultimate goal of having two deaf shelties do therapy work together was my leading force. After a great dinner at a restaurant on the St. Croix River, we got back in the car and headed to Eau Claire. The transporter from Tomah to Eau Claire arrived around 7:45 p.m. into the McDonald's parking lot where we had agreed to meet. I was so excited to meet my new little boy and couldn't wait to hug him and take him home.

I figured that Olaf had to be pretty hungry after traveling all the way from Pennsylvania to Wisconsin. I had brought along some tasty treats to help fill his tummy until we arrived at his new home. I offered a treat to Olaf, and he nearly took my finger off. My finger ached all the way back to Minnesota. I hastily loaded him up in the car, said a hearty "Thank you" to the person who had driven him from Tomah to Eau Claire, and drove him home. Thus, Olaf came into my life and became my new therapy dog challenge. I was praying I was up to the task!

CHAPTER TWO

The History of Therapy Dogs

Let's face it—we Americans are a dog-loving nation. Here are some statistics about dog ownership in the United States:

There are 1.6 dogs per household.

There are a total of 69,926,000 dogs in the United States.

The number of households owning dogs in the United States is 43,346,000.

The percentage of US households that own dogs is 36.5 percent.[1]

Wow, those are some amazing statistics. I suppose that the fact that I have six dogs pushes the number of dogs per household number up, but again, it goes to show that a human's best friend is an integral part of the American landscape. While all these dogs are performing therapy for their owners in their own way, the history of actual working therapy dogs goes back to a dog named Smoky, who is considered the first working therapy dog.

Smoky was a tiny Yorkshire terrier found abandoned in a foxhole in New Guinea in 1944. Initially, it was thought that Smoky had been abandoned by the Japanese, but Smoky didn't respond to

---

[1] https://www.avma.org/KB/Resources/Statistics/Pages/Market-research-statistics-US-pet-ownership.aspx

either Japanese or English commands. The dog was taken back to the American camp and was reportedly sold to Corporal William Wynne of Ohio for the paltry sum of $6.44—an amount that her owner needed to get back into a poker game.

Smoky and Corporal Wynne spent many combat battles together in the New Guinea theater. With her acute hearing, she warned Wynne and his fellow crew of incoming shells on the transport ship. She also performed tricks with the Special Services team often entertaining the men. Smoky even helped in building a telegraph wire at the Lingayen Gulf airbase. The wire was to be threaded through a seventy-foot-long pipe with an eight-inch diameter. The bad news was that much of the pipe was clogged with mud and other debris leaving approximately a four-inch diameter. Wynne, being the observant serviceman that he was, tied the wire to a string, which was then tied to Smoky's collar. She was asked to run through the pipe. She became frightened part of the way through and started crying. Corporal Wynne kept talking to her, soothing her and coaxing her to get to the other end of the pipe. She did it and performed a task that would have taken quite a few men to accomplish. Because she was willing to run the wire through the pipe, she helped to keep all the men and equipment in the area safe from attack.

News of Smoky's bravery made it back to the United States, and Smoky and Corporal Wynne were invited to travel to Hollywood and even overseas to perform her tricks. Smoky even got her own TV show in Cleveland, where Wynne was from. On this show she performed tricks—some of them were really difficult for the little dog, such as being blindfolded and walking on a high wire.

Smoky has been lauded as the first therapy dog because of all the visits she made visiting injured soldiers. Smoky continued visiting people in hospitals for twelve years, and sadly, at the age of fourteen, little Smoky passed away. At present there are six memorials throughout the United States honoring this brave little Yorkie.

So let's talk a little bit about the difference between service dogs and therapy dogs. Service dogs are trained to assist a human companion. This assistance can take the form of being a Seeing Eye dog, alerting to when their owner is having a seizure or a PTSD episode, opening doors and retrieving things for disabled people, sniffing out cancer at a medical facility, and the list goes on. Dogs have been pressed into service for decades often being trained as war dogs to guard, to lead, or to sniff out bombs or drugs. Service dogs play an important part in making the lives of disabled people or our veterans a much better place to live. Service dogs traditionally have been trained independent of their future owner. They are fostered as puppies in a home where they are to be taught quite a few commands. When the puppy reaches eighteen months of age, they then go to rigorous training in whatever field of assistance they are best at. This also can take a year or two, and then they are ready to meet their future handler/owner.

Therapy dogs, on the other hand, are owned and trained by their owner. They are our beloved family pets. We do all the training on our dogs, from obedience on through therapy dog training. We test with the dogs in order to receive registration/certification with one of the registering organizations. Therapy dog visits are done purely on a volunteer basis. Once we have passed the evaluation test with one of the registering organizations, we are provided with liability insurance to cover any incidents that occur, such as a resident of a facility getting hurt by the dog or tripping over a dog etc. Since dogs are animals and you never know how they'll react, it provides us peace of mind to know that at least we are not liable should someone get bitten or have an accident and get hurt.

Therapy dogs are used for emotional support for people. They can be used to help people with PTSD know that they have a best friend. People of all ages love to sink their fingers in the soft fur of a therapy dog. Therapy dogs have been used with autistic children. They can even save their owner's life, which my dogs did for me. So let's see how all this dog craziness got started.

CHAPTER THREE

Tammy, the Perfect First Dog

When I was three years old, my parents decided to get a dog. They had the house, my dad had a steady job, they had two kids, so now they needed a dog to keep up with the American Dream. My dad perused the Sunday paper, looking at advertisements for dogs for sale. You have to remember, this was the late fifties—the internet, Facebook, and Twitter were not even a far-off dream in the typical person's mind. Dad found an ad for a Shetland sheepdog for sale with a telephone number in the same exchange that ours was. Again, this was the late fifties, and you could tell the general area where a person lived by their telephone exchange. Dad called the number and heard all about shelties from the breeder. When he asked if he and my sister could go and take a look at the shelties, he found out that they lived one block over from us.

Off Dad and my sister went to check out this litter of Shetland sheepdogs. There they were—all four of them, tiny, tricolored, and absolutely adorable. Only one of the four was still available, and Linda fell in love with her—a tiny female who was the runt of the litter and displayed much adoration toward my sister as she picked her up and looked at her. Dad commented that the puppies were cute but that he had to get Linda over to Lake Nokomis for ice skating with some of her friends. As they were leaving, Dad noticed a tear in Linda's eye and turned around and told the lady, "We'll, take the damned puppy." Linda was ecstatic as they headed home with their warm bundle of fur—no ice skating after buying a puppy!

I honestly don't remember much about Tam O'Shanter or Tammy as we called her at the beginning. After all, I was only three, and the majority of my memories from my childhood all had Tammy in them. I just can't remember her as a puppy, but home movies of Tammy from back then show she was a precocious little puppy who grew up to be a fantastic family dog and guardian of the house. Since my growing-up memories have always included Tammy, I don't know what it's like to this day to live without a dog in the household. Tammy had a wealth of patience for a dog. I do remember chasing her because I wanted to pet her but usually ended up catching her tail as she tried to get away from my reaching fingers. She never did snap at me for pulling her tail. To this day, I wish I could tell Tammy how sorry I am that I pulled her tail. Yes, I was young, but she was such a great dog and she deserved better than that.

Tammy was a fantastic friend to me growing up—well, at least as far as eating some of Mom's cooking was concerned. I was a picky eater as a kid. My mom did the best she could as a cook and prepared meals for the family every night. But being such a picky eater, I often didn't want to eat certain items on my plate. That's where Tammy became such a good friend. She knew from years of experience that more than likely I would slide something off my plate onto the floor for her. And Tammy would inhale whatever was tossed her way like a Hoover vacuum picking up spills off the carpet. My parents were adamant also that we had to eat everything on our plate before we could leave the table and go back outside to play with our friends. My sister and I were daily reminded that there were starving people in China who would love to have the food that she had prepared for us. I always thought to myself that maybe she could box it up and ship it to these starving people, but sassing back was definitely not tolerated in our home. So I crammed the food into my mouth and forced it down because I wanted to get back outside and play with my friends.

One of the things that Mom cooked that I absolutely detested was yellow pea soup. Mom would soak the yellow peas in water for a couple of days (I assume to soften them up) before throwing them in a big pot, along with some ham and carrots and water, to make the soup. Inevitably, those darn peas would still be hard even after soaking and cooking them. I hated Mom's pea soup, but I wasn't bright enough to figure out that cold pea soup is worse than hot pea soup. I would fidget at the table and hoped Mom would look away so I could plop down some of the pea soup for Tammy to scarf up. Sometimes it worked; sometimes it didn't. I remember many times when I had to eat cold pea soup in order to get back outside to spend another couple of hours playing with my friends. Yes, Tammy was quite a food-weather friend back in those days, and I really appreciated how she saved me from having to eat some things that I really didn't want to eat.

As I grew older, Tammy became one of my best friends although it was Dad whom she had wrapped around her little paw. Those two had this unbreakable bond, and I know Dad was devastated when Tammy eventually died. But even though Tammy and Dad did share a special bond, Tammy, being the great friend that she was, would often sleep under the covers with me at night. She must have roasted under the covers, but she always dove underneath, snuggling in around my feet to keep them warm in the winter.

Tammy never went through any obedience courses. I don't think our family was cognizant of training dogs back then. And training methods back then were pretty harsh with prong and choke collars used on all dogs. Tammy would probably have been mortified if we had used a prong collar on her. We used a simple leather buckle collar on Tammy.

In the wintertime, the postal worker would wear a path through the snow about six to eight feet from the front door. This saved him from having to walk down each front walk, along the sidewalk and back up the front walk of the next house. It really lessened the number of steps he had to make to deliver mail. Winter afternoons after I got home from school, I would hook Tammy up to the leash, and we would run up and down the well-worn path that the mail carrier had made. Tammy would run ahead of me as if pulling me on a sled, and I used the leash like reins on a horse. Oftentimes, I would get back home wheezing from the exertion but loving every second of it.

My dad had a pretty heavy cigarette-smoking habit back in the day. In fact, he had a three-pack-a-day habit. I still remember the red-and-white Winston packs that he smoked. He didn't like the boxes; he liked the soft packs. When he had smoked all twenty cigarettes out of the pack, the package became a toy for Tammy to chase. We have home movies of Tammy running to catch a Winston pack as it sailed through the air. She loved to chew them and cause the cellophane wrapper on the package to crinkle and make noise. God forbid that anyone should do that nowadays. It would probably be considered dog abuse, but Tammy loved chasing those cellophane cigarette packs.

I was raised in your typical middle-class family in the 1950s and 1960s. We always had shelter, food, and clothing. We might not have had everything we wanted, but my parents were always there for my sister and me, and we knew they loved us. Both my parents taught us right from wrong, and Mom took us to Sunday school every week. Mom was also very involved in PTA, and she was a Brownie and Girl Scout leader and also chaperoned school dances. As an adult, I am so appreciative that she was so involved in our lives, but as a kid, there were many times I felt stifled because Mom was leading or chaperoning an event.

From birth, I was a tomboy. I rarely played with dolls, preferring a cowboy hat and a six-shooter strapped to my waist. Every time I drew my gun, the barrel would fall open. My parents purchased stick horses for me to ride because I was always running as a kid and I loved horses. I can't even begin to count the number of stick horses I wore out. When I ran out of stick horses, I grabbed my mom's broom and galloped up the street, using that as my steady steed.

My mom was not always thrilled that I was such a tomboy. I remember a Girl Scout event at my grade school when I was in fifth grade. Mom was the scout leader, and she wanted us to prepare a nice afternoon tea for the scout's mothers. We were dressed nicely in dresses and Mary Jane patent leather shoes. We had made dainty teacakes and had several pots of tea on the stove. When we were all ready to serve our guests, my mom asked me to get the moms to the table. Out I walked where all the moms had gathered and yelled "Come and get it!" My mom was mortified. Turning her youngest daughter into a lady was becoming a distant glimmer in her eyes.

We attended a Lutheran church, which was part of the LCA synod back then. I used to call it the "party" synod since the rules were not as strict as those as some of the other Lutheran synods. I loved to sing but didn't feel that I had a very good voice, so I never participated in junior or senior high school choirs. I did, however, belong to choir at our church and sang in one of their choirs from the age of ten until forty, when I chose to drop my membership in the church because of the driving distance from home. I do remember singing in the Senior Choir and practicing every Wednesday evening for Sunday's service and for special concerts. I was friends and neighbors with many of the choir members, and we would sit around after choir, telling jokes, drinking coffee, and just laughing about some of the funny antics of humans in our world. While choir was a volunteer effort for me, I had no interest in volunteering in any other capacity in the church. I was still a self-centered young adult.

My mom allowed me to start dating at the age of sixteen. Tammy was my touchstone in the dating world. If Tammy liked a guy I was dating, I knew he was an okay guy. However, if she didn't like him, I also knew it was time to say adieu. She had such a way of getting to the heart of people and what made them tick. She always had my best interests at heart, and I loved her for that because, in every case when she was indifferent or even agitated with one of my dates, she was 100 percent right every time. Actually, it's still that way in my life now with my dogs—if they have an issue with someone, there's usually a good reason for it. At an early age, I learned that dogs can be a great judge of the human character—much better than my own judgment when it comes to some people.

Tammy became ill when she was twelve years old. In a dog her size, the uterus should be about the size of a small pencil. In her case, it had swollen to the size of a man's arm. The local veterinarian wanted $100 to perform surgery to remove her uterus. Again, my dad was hesitant because of the cost, but both my sister and I cried and begged him to allow Tammy to have the surgery. It was at this point that I realized that Tammy was actually a part of the family. I have to admit that I had had the mind-set for a long time as a kid that Tammy was just a dog. But when the very real possibility existed that Tammy might die, it really brought home the fact that I thought of her as my little sister—the little sister I never had. Dad relented with three crying females haranguing him. Tammy had the surgery and lived four more years, dying in my arms at the age of sixteen. I thought I had lost my best friend, but I also knew she had been suffering in the months before she died. She had been having much difficulty breathing, and while I hated to lose my little four-legged sister, I knew she had earned her passage to the Rainbow Bridge.

Tammy taught me a lot about caring for another animal and how much a part of the family a dog does become. While I wasn't the "model owner" with Tammy, she had enough patience and love to put up with my childhood antics of pulling her tail and chasing her. She was the perfect dog for me growing up, and I still miss her to this day.

CHAPTER FOUR

Brandy and Tanya

Tammy's death left such a void in my whole family's life. Poor Tammy hadn't even been gone a week when one day my mom asked me if I wanted to go to a local pet shop to look at some sheltie puppies. I gave a resounding yes, so off we went to look at puppies. There were four cute sable sheltie puppies in a playpen in the center of the shop. I played with them all, but one of them kept trying to get out of the playpen so I could hold him in my arms. He was sweet, energetic, and Mom decided to buy him on the spot. Dad was working up at his hardware store as usual, so Mom and I drove over there to show him our newest family member. Dad had his back to us when we went in the store and was talking to one of the employees. When I approached him holding that sweet bundle of puppy love and said "Dad," he turned around and held the puppy like he was a fragile child. Dad said he knew we had gotten a puppy the minute I said "Dad" when I walked up behind him.

We named the new puppy Brandy. He was a rich shade of deep red sable with very little white on him. Brandy brought so much joy to our household especially after the loss of Tammy. There was no one Brandy met that he didn't love. He was to this day the friendliest sheltie I've ever had the pleasure to know in my life.

My dad was a travelling salesman up until I reached my senior year in high school. At that time, he purchased a hardware store, and he and my mom worked at the store. Because he was on the road five days a week during most of my growing-up years, Mom was the one who actually raised my sister and I, and she was there 24-7.

After I graduated from high school, I was very motivated to start at the University of Minnesota. Dad had just purchased the hardware store, so they were not able to give me any help with college. The University of Minnesota was the cheapest alternative at that time, so I chose to go there and live at home. I had decided to have a double major in French education and park and recreation. I started summer session at the U of M the week after I graduated. I had attended a high school with 850 graduates in my class alone, so I was used to a large school. But I wasn't prepared for the size of the university.

My first class of summer session was a French class. I was really nervous going into the class. The U of M was so intimidating both in the size of the campus and the number of students. I forced myself into my first French class, expecting to be totally overwhelmed, but instead the professor starting writing some words in French on the blackboard. He turned around to face the class and said, "I know you all want to know how to swear in French. Here they are. Better write them down because I won't be posting this again." Being that some of the words coming out of my mouth could make even a sailor blush, I thought this was totally cool and proceeded to write them all down. Unfortunately, swearing in French is the only thing I remember well from all the French classes I took at the U of M. Well, at least I remember something!

I was nineteen and attending the U when Brandy came into my life. I was doing the dating thing but hadn't found anyone who interested me much. Back in the seventies, it was common to go to bars to listen to live music and dance to the music on weekends. One Saturday evening, one of my girlfriends and I went to the Bronco Bar, which was located in the Chanhassen Dinner Theater complex. We went to hear a particular band. While there, I noticed a guy standing at the bar who looked like Robert Redford. I decided to mosey on up to the bar and order a drink and try to get the Robert Redford look-alike's attention. After ordering my drink, the guy on the other side of me from Robert Redford asked me a question. He wasn't Robert Redford, but he was handsome in his own right. We started up a conversation and spent the whole evening together, dancing. And that is where I met my future husband, Glen.

Glen loved dogs but really was not too keen on shelties. It seems that a neighbor of his had had a sheltie when he was growing up. This sheltie was left outside in the backyard and did as many shelties are known to do—it ran circles in the yard and barked constantly. The poor dog was bored, but Glen didn't know that being a kid. All he knew was that this dog was very obnoxious, and of course, that had colored his opinion of all shelties. But then he met Brandy. Glen was so impressed with Brandy and his friendliness that all his negative thoughts about shelties disappeared.

I still had not entered the world of dog training yet. Brandy was fun to take on walks and was such a loving dog that obedience really wasn't an issue—well, it became an issue whenever my parents had people over for a backyard party. Because of Brandy's great love for people, he tended to jump up on them whenever anyone came in the yard or house. Since I hadn't been involved in the dog-training arena yet, I didn't know how to stop Brandy from doing that. The jumping up on people problem would rear its ugly head later in my life with one of my collies.

Brandy helped to solidify my own love for Shetland sheepdogs. He had this upbeat attitude and he was always thrilled when I came home from school every day. One summer when I was in my early twenties, I was one of the counselors on a church choir camping trip. We had been gone only for a week, but when my parents came down to pick me up when we arrived back home, Brandy tried jumping out of my mom's arms in his quest to get to me. It caused quite a few smiles on the choristers' and counselors' faces, watching Brandy try to get to me to show how much he had missed me. Honestly, how can you possibly have a bad day when a warm bundle of fur is so eager to greet you and show its loyalty and love for you after you've been away?

Glen and I dated for a year and half before getting engaged. Glen bought me a beautiful apricot-colored sheltie puppy from a store called Zayre Shoppers City. Tanya was beautiful with her apricot sable fur and lots of white on her face and a full white collar.

However, Tanya was a typical puppy mill sheltie. I didn't know anything about puppy mills back then. Poor Tanya was scared of her own shadow and often cowered under a chair when a plane went overhead as my parents lived close to one of the runways of the MSP airport.

Thank God we had Brandy in the household, so Tanya had another stable, strong dog to show her the ropes of what it means to be a loved dog. Tanya and Brandy bonded in another way also. The day after I got married, Tanya gave birth to five adorable sable-and-white male puppies. We had names for each of them and found good homes for four of the pups and decided to keep the one little boy with the full white collar. We asked my parents if they wanted to keep Tanya as she had grown so comfortable being in their home with Brandy as her mentor, and they said yes, they wanted to keep her. When our little puppy whom we had named Angus was old enough, we took him home. My adventure with shelties was continuing.

CHAPTER FIVE

Angus, Heather, Blue, and Carly

Angus was as sweet-natured as his father, Brandy, was. He had a few puppy adventures that gave us pause during his first year with us. He acquired the nickname Mr. Steak one evening. One of our wedding gifts was a tabletop meat broiler, so we settled down one evening with steak for dinner. After about five minutes, Glen and I realized that Angus was not in the living room with us begging for food. I snuck into the kitchen and found Angus had grabbed the huge hunk of steak that was still on the broiler and was happily munching it down. He also gained the nickname Butter Boy when he grabbed a full stick of butter off the counter and inhaled it—paper and all. Little did I know that Angus was priming me for some of the ultimate counter surfers—collies! For the most part, though, he was a wonderful dog, and we couldn't wait to move into a house so Angus could have the run of the backyard.

Glen was and is a good person. He came from a middle-class background the same as I did. But he had a dysfunctional homelife growing up. His parents' first child, a daughter, died in childbirth with the umbilical cord wrapped around her neck, and a doctor that wasn't willing to get off the golf course in time to save the baby. They tried again, and this time, a baby boy, Danny, was born. Glen arrived three years later.

Danny was an exceptionally bright child with a very high IQ. Glen's mom later told me that there were signs that maybe they should have seen. Danny was a perfectionist, and if he couldn't pitch a perfect no-hitter game, he often had a meltdown. They were able to let Danny babysit Glen at an early age—when Danny was nine years old. Danny was a very responsible and adultlike child. Glen's dad focused his whole attention on Danny since Danny's birth. I understand their joy with Danny's birth after losing their first child in childbirth.

When Danny turned twelve years old, he grew six inches in six months, and that growth spurt seemed to throw his whole body chemistry out of whack. Danny started sinking into schizophrenia. Glen's parents took him to a myriad number of doctors, trying to find answers for Danny and to help him become "normal" again. This was back in the early 1960s, and treatment options included strong drugs and shock treatments to his brain. Nothing medically helped, and his parents sought answers through religion and spirituality. Unfortunately, they became involved with a cultlike religion, but they were able to extricate themselves from the group in the late 1970s. But while they were involved, it did give them some comfort to hear that Danny's soul was going through the trials in this lifetime because of a former life where Danny had been supposedly evil. I can only imagine the hell his parents went through trying to find answers for their son, whom they adored and loved.

All the attention put on Danny left Glen on his own quite a bit. Thankfully, a cousin took him under his wing and taught him how to hunt, fish, and trap. I honestly think that, if Glen had not turned to those things, he might have had a very different life story. He could so easily have gotten in with a bad crowd and been involved in drugs and mischief.

When I got married, I knew all about Glen's family and past. However, I wasn't developed enough or cognizant enough to understand how his upbringing impacted his life as an adult. I honestly think I was more in love with the idea of being in love and getting married than truly loving the man who became my husband, and for that I apologize from my heart to Glen.

Major fissures surfaced within the first year of our marriage. We had only been married for two months when Glen came home and announced that he was going to go out west backpacking for a couple of weeks with a "friend" I had never heard of before. I had the expectation that Glen and I would be taking a vacation together. Glen justified his backpacking trip by saying that he had always wanted to make such a trip into the Rockies. Granted we had only dated for two and one half years before we got married, but you would think that something that important would have been mentioned to the person you were going to marry. But Glen was silent about his needs, wants, and expectations. He went on the trip despite my objections. I was hurt and resentful, and that confrontation started a series of resentments in our marriage.

We did move into our first home before we had our first anniversary. Since both of us worked outside the home, we thought it would be good to get Angus a companion, so Heather Kay joined the family. Heather was a tiny sable sheltie, but despite being such a little girl, she had one of the biggest personalities I had seen in a dog. Glen was completely enamored with Heather. Despite the fact that Heather had strewn the contents of a big garbage can throughout the house while we were gone at a Christmas concert, he just couldn't get mad at her; she was just too cute.

While we were still living in the apartment, I had taken Angus to obedience classes. This was still the day and age of dominating dogs instead of rewarding dogs for good behavior. I was appalled at a couple of the classes when the instructor "hung" a couple of the dogs that were showing belligerent behavior. Hanging a dog involves lifting the dog by its collar off its feet. I'm guessing it was used to show dominance over the dog, but I was totally shocked whenever a dog was hung in class. I was so grateful that Angus was so willing to do whatever I asked of him that hanging was not an option. But seeing the dogs hung by their collars left such a nasty taste in my mouth that I decided not to follow up with additional obedience classes and definitely no classes for Heather as she was even more sensitive than Angus was.

We moved around quite a bit the first ten years of our marriage. Our first house was in Farmington. I resented the drive into Bloomington where I worked. This was before they had made any improvements to 35W or Cedar Avenue. Oftentimes I got stuck in bumper-to-bumper traffic, and it would take me over an hour and a half to get home from Bloomington to Farmington.

We decided to move after a year in our first house. We moved up to the suburb of Richfield into a cute 1949 cottage in the west Richfield area. The house had a lot of character but had a fatal flaw—the basement leaked every time it rained. We decided to move in to Bloomington, where Glen had grown up. We purchased a nice three-bedroom rambler and lived there with Angus and Heather for several years.

The years passed, and Glen and I thought of Angus and Heather as our children since we had been unable to have any children. Yet even though I had these two wonderful dogs living in the household, it still had not crossed my mind to partner with them to visit people who were shut in or lonely or ill. I was still a very self-absorbed human being.

Glen and I had been married almost ten years when major fractures continued to occur in our marriage. We had been drifting apart for quite some time, but neither of us seemed able to make the decision to divorce. I just did not have the strength of character it took to make the decision to divorce at that time. I honestly did not feel loved or appreciated in my marriage though.

Glen had suffered a couple of losses during this time. His mom passed away at age sixty-two. He and his mom were very close, and losing her was devastating to Glen. Glen had been suffering from a back injury that occurred around the time that his mom passed away. He seemed to withdraw further and further away from me. I was feeling desperate to be loved, and Glen seemed unable to provide me with the love and attention I so craved. So what did I do? I had an affair with one of my coworkers. To protect his identity, I'll call him Tom.

Tom came from a middle-class lifestyle as I did, and he was married and had a three-year-old child and an infant baby girl when we started our affair. Like many people who have affairs, we justified our relationship by explaining how neglected and misunderstood we were at home. Tom had worked with me when I first started at

Sperry. I found him to be very kind and patient in teaching me the ins and outs of Sperry's computer program.

Our friendship and status as colleagues lasted for five years, but in 1986, something changed. We started out having lunch together as friends, but the more we got to know each other, the more we both started falling in love. Oh yes, the affair was exciting and exhilarating at first. Just as new love always brings a rush of feelings and emotions at the beginning, so too did our affair bring the same sort of excitement even though we couldn't share with anyone that we were in a full-fledged affair.

The relationship between Glen and me was so distant when the affair with Tom started. Tom filled such a huge void in my life and showered me with love and attention. But of course that attention only lasted during the daytime hours. At night we each went home to our spouses. I was walking a tightrope for the first couple of years of the affair, enjoying all the love and affection that Tom was giving me yet coming home and playacting as if nothing in my life were different. This was so not how I was raised. The moral issue of what I was doing weighed heavily on me. My parents would have been so disappointed in me if they had found out about my affair—well, my mother would have been disappointed, but I truly think my dad would have understood. But I didn't feel I could talk to either of them about what was happening in my life.

As far as I know, Glen knew nothing about the affair. I was far too good at lying and covering up. When I would get home from one of my trysts, I felt an enormous amount of guilt over cheating on Glen but not enough to make me stop. I felt guilty too about being away from home so much, and being away from my dogs that always seemed to help ground me. Glen never questioned me about why I was gone so much, and in my jaundiced eyes, he didn't seem to care. So the affair continued off and on for nineteen years.

At the same time that my affair started, I was trying desperately to find some common ground in our marriage. I thought that moving to a smaller town and restoring an old Victorian house would provide the challenge and direction I was seeking. We eventually bought an old Victorian house in Carver, Minnesota. Restoring the old Victorian and using it as a bed-and-breakfast inn was the plan. I was still working in the Twin Cities, and Glen ran into Chaska often for business, so we sometimes had local contractors come in and work on various parts of the restoration. One day, one of the electricians working on the house was in the house alone. When he went outside to get additional tools from his truck, Angus ran out the back door. We hadn't fenced in the yard yet, so Angus was able to get away from the house. The electrician tried calling him and chasing him, and that was probably the worst thing that could have happened. Angus got up onto the highway and was struck and killed by a passing semitruck.

We were devastated. Angus was like our firstborn child, and to have him die so horrendously took us a long time to get over. A neighbor in Carver was a breeder of shelties, and she felt so bad for us over the loss of Angus that she offered a beautiful blue merle puppy to us. Merle is a color phase of several breeds—collie, Shetland sheepdog, Australian shepherd, among others. The merle coat color produces mottled patches of color on the dog's coat.

Blueberry, or Blue, as we called him, came into our lives. Blue was a sweet dog, somewhat shy, but he definitely loved us. A little more than a year later, I purchased another blue merle puppy from the Carver breeder. Carly Simone had bright blue eyes and was probably one of the cutest puppies I had ever seen. Everyone commented on how cute she was, and when she would look up at you with those big blue eyes, you couldn't help but melt, and extra treats would come her way!

We eventually finished the old Victorian house, fenced in the backyard, and did run it as a bed-and-breakfast. It was difficult for us though as we had to give up our bedroom for guests and sleep downstairs on the hide-a-bed sofa in the back parlor. It was difficult too to keep the dogs quiet all the time as they would hear activity upstairs and think there were burglars in the house. Eventually, in 1991 we stopped using the house as a bed-and-breakfast, and it became our house again. However, the fractures in our marriage were still there, but we didn't speak of them.

Life went on with the three shelties—Heather, Blue, and Carly—and our part-time marriage limped along also. In December of 1991, I felt nauseous a good deal of every day and was extremely tired. I have an ulcer, so I figured that my ulcer was bleeding again. My menstrual cycle had always been so regular, but in December of 1991, I had missed two periods. After fourteen years of marriage without getting pregnant, I laughed off the possibility that I was pregnant. I bought a home pregnancy test, took it, and was shocked to discover that I was pregnant. I called up my best friend and begged her to tell me that it was possible to get a false positive on a pregnancy test. She said that I was more likely to get a false negative than a false positive. I was in total shock. How could I possibly be pregnant after fourteen years of marriage and five years of an affair with unprotected sex resulting in no pregnancy?

My mind was in shock and was totally numb after taking the test. Having an abortion was not an option. I just could not kill a baby to protect Glen from finding out that I had been having an affair. I made an appointment right away with my gynecologist and found out that, yes, I was pregnant. They did an ultrasound because I was fairly high-risk, being thirty-seven and a first pregnancy. They also gave me a prescription for prenatal vitamins and told me I should get more rest and scheduled another ultrasound for early January.

I spent that Christmas in a haze, feeling completely exhausted and still unable to keep much food down. I remember driving to work that December feeling numb and often reaching my workplace without any memory of the drive in. I was in a quandary over what would happen if the baby was born with dark hair and brown eyes and looking nothing like my husband. Everyone at my workplace and my whole family were so excited for me, but I just couldn't get excited. If this pregnancy had happened just five years before this, everything would have been so exciting.

I went in for an ultrasound in early January. The fetus was not moving and had not grown at all since the first ultrasound. The doctors said that the baby had died. They explained that many women have miscarriages and its often nature's way of terminating a pregnancy that is not tenable to go full term. My options were to allow the fetus to spontaneously abort or to have a D & C.

If I thought I had been in a haze since finding out I was pregnant, the fog deepened, and I couldn't come to grips with what was happening. I opted for the D & C, and Glen came with me to the procedure. I was in such major shock over everything that had happened to me, my body, and to Glen that I was like an automaton nodding yes or no to questions asked of me by the hospital. The procedure was done, and I rode home deep in a fog of silence. Glen was totally devastated by the loss of the baby. Because I didn't show a lot of emotion to him about the baby, he assumed I didn't care and hadn't loved the baby. But he was so wrong.

I cried myself to sleep many nights over the loss of the only baby that I might have had. I was so conflicted after the D & C. I was relieved that I wouldn't have to tell Glen about my affair and totally devastated at having to manually terminate the only pregnancy that seemed to take. My dogs knew that I was sinking into a depression of sorts, and they would often snuggle up next to me while I cried. As time wore on that winter, though, I did what I have always done. I dusted myself off, went back to work, and tried to carry on. That little baby has never left my consciousness though. As I write this, he would have been twenty-three going on twenty-four, and who knows? Maybe he would be a father. But we'll never know as that wasn't in the grand scheme of my life.

I kept at my job in Minneapolis as I truly did enjoy the job and the people I worked with. But I was feeling very restless after the loss of the baby. My soul knew that having a baby was not going to be an option in my life. Glen was unwilling to adopt "someone else's kid" as he put it, and I was never able to have and sustain a pregnancy. My restlessness turned into a yearning to live on a hobby farm, away from the mass of civilization that was Minneapolis, where I worked every day, and out in open country, where maybe I could get some farm animals—horses in particular. I had never outgrown my love of horses, and I fondly remembered all the stick horses I had worn out.

After work I would frequently drive out in the country away from the town of Carver, where we were currently living. One winter day, I drove along the road fronting the Minnesota River and turned off on a winding road that climbed to the top of the river bluffs. I took this road about half a mile from the bluffs and found a parcel of land with an old house and a Quonset hut on it. I wondered if the owner would parcel off five or ten acres with the house and Quonset hut on it. I went to the county seat and found out who the owner of the land was. I gave him a call.

He was a very nice man, and he said that the old house was actually one of the original log homes built in that area in the 1860s or 1870s. Both Glen and I loved log homes, and to own a vintage log home with history was exciting. The owner allowed us to enter the house and explore it. We had visions of removing the horizontal siding covering up the big square hand-hewn logs and removing some of the plaster and lath inside also to expose the beautiful logs.

The house was fairly simple in design with three rooms downstairs—living room, kitchen, and bathroom—and two bedrooms upstairs. The house seemed solidly constructed at the time. As we made plans to sell our house in Carver, winter passed over to spring. One bright, sunny Sunday, we drove out to see the old log house and continue with our plans for restoration. We went upstairs to talk about how we were going to reconstruct the bedrooms when we realized that we could make the whole house sway just by rocking back and forth. When we had been out to the log house previously, it was winter, and I'm sure all the logs and timbers were frozen. But once warmer weather melted all the frozen logs, it was obvious that the house was not structurally sound. Neither of us had any knowledge or experience in shoring up log homes or even if it was possible. Unfortunately, the house had been abandoned for too many years, and decades of neglect had taken their toll on this historic old structure. It broke my heart, but we had to back out of the deal.

We turned our attention to a parcel of land closer to the bluffs on the same road. We contacted the owner and found out he was willing to parcel off 10 acres for us from his larger 280 acres. We decided to build a new house and found a Cape Cod open floor plan and a builder in Jordan who was building the same house. We purchased the parcel and hired the builder, and by fall of 1993, our house was ready to move in to. Hobby farm living on the prairie was just beginning!

CHAPTER SIX

Life on the Hobby Farm

We started our hobby farm adventure by moving in on Halloween 1993. We had no garage or outbuildings yet, nor did we have any fencing for the dogs. That would come next spring. We settled in to our new home and tried to get to know the neighbors living on our same road. We had a big surprise waiting for us though. Both neighbors across the road were alcoholics. One of them was a belligerent drunk. He didn't want to see new people moving in and would sometimes take pot shots with his rifle if people stepped onto his property. What the heck had we gotten into? Eventually, these neighbors got used to the fact that we had moved in and weren't going to be intimidated into moving out!

We named our little hobby farm Wild Prairie Farm. The winter of 1993/'94 was much colder than normal, and I can still remember starting my truck at six o'clock in the morning and freezing my tush off driving to work. Eventually, winter gave way to spring, so we built a pole barn garage and fenced in the backyard so the dogs could have some room to run.

That same winter, Heather, who was sixteen years old by now, started having breathing issues. One evening, we had to race her to the emergency vet's office. He gave her some medication to help with her breathing, but she died in Glen's arms on the way back home. Suffice it to say, we were both devastated at the loss of Heather, but Glen especially so. Since the first day we brought her home, he had such a bond with her, and he was having difficulty dealing with her death.

Heather died around the time of our anniversary, so on the quiet, I purchased a sable-and-white collie puppy, Tawney. I knew we couldn't replace Heather, and it would be unfair to put that kind of burden on a sheltie puppy, but a collie was a totally different animal. At the same time, Glen had finagled a blue merle puppy girl from our former neighbor in Carver. So in the same day, Sybil, the little blue merle sheltie, and Tawney, the sable-and-white collie, entered our lives.

Sybil was named Sybil for a reason—she had so many personalities. She looked like a little bumblebee and seemed as angry as a hornet when you would approach her to pet her. She would grumble and growl when you held her. Over time, she became much more approachable as we socialized her with other dogs and people. But until her death, she was always a little spitfire and ornery little girl.

Tawney, the collie, was another matter. She was as kind as the day was long. Her collie nose grew and grew almost like Pinocchio's, and my nieces used to call her anteater because of her long nose. That was my first experience raising a collie, and the differences between collies and shelties became very apparent to me working with Tawney. I did not take either Tawney or Sybil through obedience classes as we had fenced off a large portion of our backyard on the hobby farm for the dogs to run. The dogs loved running out back all day long, barking at the horses grazing in the backyard.

In the mid-1990s, I had such a longing for something to fill my life with purpose. Obviously, something was and had been missing in my life. All my friends had kids and were so busy raising their children that I often felt left out whenever we would get together and discuss life. My marriage was running lukewarm as Glen had had a myriad of back problems starting ten years previous, and these back problems kept getting worse and worse. And I had backed off of my affair with Tom since he had gotten married on the rebound to a girl he met after I had turned his marriage proposal down for the umpteenth time. I was adrift trying to figure out what I could do with my life that would make it have meaning.

As had been pretty typical throughout my life, I figured "acquiring" something would help ease my loneliness. I had had a love of all things horses since a kid and had spent many a Saturday morning watching Roy Rogers and Trigger, Dale Evans and Buttermilk, the Lone Ranger with Silver, and Hopalong Cassidy with his horse, Topper. These silver-screen stars were my idols, and I needed a horse of my own to keep up with them. My sister had a teacher friend who had two Arabian horses he wanted to sell. He was willing to trade the two horses for my 1986 Ford Mustang convertible. He told me the bay horse, Lani, was twelve years old and her daughter, the gray Ali, was five years old. I made the deal and took the horses down from northern Minnesota to a boarding stable near Belle Plaine. Once the Arabian registry paperwork arrived, I found out that Lani was actually sixteen and Ali was eleven. Lani, who was really a sweet horse, had hock issues related to arthritis and injuries she had sustained when younger. And Ali was so barn sour that I couldn't ride her out of the boarding facility without "Mom" along. I had made a big mistake buying these horses without really knowing what I was getting into.

Eventually, I traded the two mares who actually were out of old Polish Arabian bloodlines. What I got was a two-year-old black Arabian cross. She was a nice girl but definitely not for a total novice to horses as I was. I ended up selling her at auction.

I still wanted a horse though. Since I was over forty at the time I got my first horse, I decided to look into getting a gaited horse. A gaited horse moves in an ambling fashion and is smooth to ride, while a trotting horse moves in a two-beat rhythm with diagonal legs working in tandem. The gaited horses have their own unique way of moving and are much smoother than your typical trotting horse. I looked at them all—Tennessee Walkers, Rocky Mountains, Paso Finos, Missouri Fox Trotters, and finally, Peruvian Pasos. I visited a Peruvian Paso breeding ranch in Mankato, and I was so impressed with the fact that I could walk right into the stallion's stall and hug him. He was as gentle as a lamb. I made a deal with the owner to purchase a beautiful bright-red chestnut gelding, Tengo Arrogante, and a more-subdued chestnut filly named Alajandra. Finally, I had found the breed of horse that was best for me.

I started riding Tengo all the time and eventually joined a riding club based out of Mankato. We did drill exhibits at the Minnesota Horse Expo every year. I loved riding drill because I love to perform. Eventually, I purchased two more mares and a stallion, Vaquero. Vaquero was a beautiful buckskin color, and his fur shimmered in the sun. He had a big white blaze and four white socks. He was beautiful. One of the mares I purchased, Anna Maria Mia, was a well-built black mare out of some wonderful old Peruvian Paso bloodlines. She and Vaquero produced some gorgeous babies together.

Life went on at the farm. We lost both Blue and Carly within a year of each other. Both of them had been such wonderful dogs, giving both Glen and me unconditional love whenever either of us was down. My parents purchased a little tricolor sheltie in 1996 that they had named Cappy (short for Captain). However, my dad called me up one day and asked if they could take Cappy out to the farm so he could live out there. Apparently, my mom was developing Alzheimer's disease and wasn't able to care for this sweet little puppy, and my dad was covering up for Mom so that my sister and I wouldn't know how bad Mom was. I didn't have a clue at that time that Mom was developing Alzheimer's, and I thought it strange that Mom didn't want to care for such a cute little puppy. But of course I told him to take Cappy out. Cappy was a sweet, sweet dog and fit right in with Sybil and Tawney. In fact, he fit in too well with Sybil because, in June of 1997, Sybil gave birth to three little tricolor shelties, two males and one female.

When the puppies were about three weeks old, a severe thunderstorm with possible tornados was forecast on a Sunday afternoon in July. I was on the farm by myself—Glen was in California on business. The horses in the pasture area were acting very strangely, so I put them into the horse barn. The sky grew progressively darker, and the air was so sticky. About four o'clock in the afternoon, the sky turned a weird green color, and everything became still. I knew the farm was probably in the path of a severe storm, so I grabbed all six dogs (Cappy, Sybil, Tawney, and the three puppies) and raced downstairs with them.

Our house had a walkout basement, which faced north, so I knew where the west corner of the basement was located. I had always heard to go to the southwest corner of the basement so I rushed to get all of us down into that corner. It began to rain and the wind blew so hard that I couldn't even see more than three feet out the back sliding-glass doors. It was a real effort to keep the dogs calm. Poor Tawney was so frightened that she literally tried to crawl on me, and if she could have, she probably would have crawled into my skin.

After about ten minutes, things settled down, so the dogs and I all crept upstairs to see if there had been any damage. The house itself seemed fine—no broken windows, shutters blown off, no shingles missing. However, when I walked out the front door, I couldn't believe my eyes. About fifty feet from the edge of the house, we had built the pole barn garage. Next to the garage was the horse barn—also a pole building. When I walked outside, the garage was no longer there. The tornado had lifted the building and whipped the metal siding and roof along with the pole supports over to Scott County across the river.

I am so thankful that the tornado took the garage instead of the house or the horse barn with all the horses inside. I had only a very basic cell phone at that time, so I called my parents and told them that they needed to let Glen know that a tornado had blown our garage away. My parents were supposed to pick him up at the airport the next day. They were concerned about me, but I told them that I was fine but that I had no electricity in the house. The tornado had ripped all the electrical wires between the house and garage. Neighbors came over to help me, and they shut down the whole electrical system in case there were any live wires hanging in the garage or near the house. That was a good thing. We had some newborn barn kitties that had taken up residence in the garage under a big pile of wood that was going to be used for horse stalls. I rushed out to make sure they were okay and, in my haste, almost stepped on an electric wire. If the power hadn't been shut down, that could have been disastrous.

Once everything settled down after the tornado, we had the garage rebuilt, only this time using a different company that seemed to make a better product. The puppies continued to grow and thrive that summer. We gave one of the male puppies to a friend of ours and kept the other two. We had Spotty, a little tricolor female with a tiny white spot in the black fur of her back, and Teddybear, a male tricolor with a full collar and sweet personality. We rehomed Cappy to an elderly woman who absolutely adored him, and I honestly think having Cappy in her life kept her more vital and active than her kids had thought possible. It was a good match for both of them.

In the late 1990s, Glen's back issues kept getting worse. He was constantly in pain, and his quality of life was not very good. Unfortunately, that translated to our quality of life as a couple not being very good. The original back injury had occurred at his workplace back in the early 1980s. The doctors tried many things to help relieve the pain—physical therapy, strengthening exercises, antidepressants, and of course, painkiller medication. Nothing seemed to be working, and his only recourse was to undergo spinal fusion surgery.

At the end of January 2000, Glen had his back surgery. The surgery was quite long and required them to go in from the back and the front to stabilize the spine with both cadaver bone and titanium rods. After surgery, Glen seemed to always be in pain. When I suggested that maybe it was pain from the surgery and to give it some time to heal, he adamantly said that wasn't the problem. He was sure they had damaged a nerve during the surgery. Whatever the cause of the pain, the result was still the same—copious amounts of painkillers. Many of the traditional painkillers didn't seem to work, but they finally ended up putting him on fentanyl patches. Fentanyl is a narcotic pain medication with a high risk of addiction and is what end-stage cancer patients are given for pain. That pretty much is the end of the line when it comes to painkillers.

Along with the strong painkillers, the doctors gave Glen antidepressants and antianxiety medication. Obviously, their thinking was that he had to be depressed and stressed out not being able to work, but I'm pretty sure the doctors had no clue how fentanyl and the various antianxiety and depression drugs worked when taken together. Glen's personality totally changed. His whole life at that point was consumed with his pain and making sure he was able to get his next batch of fentanyl patches. These drugs are so restricted by the FDA that the doctor cannot call in a refill. The patient has to visit the doctor and get a signed prescription each month.

From the mid-1990s through the early 2000s, my affair had really slacked off. He had gotten remarried to a woman on the rebound when I continually turned down his marriage proposals, plus he had had a son with her. I didn't want to interfere at all with their relationship although he called me quite a bit and we met for lunch several times. He was very unhappy in this marriage and asked me for advice. I wanted to tell him to run away from the marriage as he didn't seem at all happy, but there was now a baby involved, so I didn't give him any advice. The chemistry was still there between us, but so much time and major life events had happened to each of us that it was difficult to even see each other or imagine a life together. Whenever we would get together for lunch, I looked at him and felt in my heart that I could really be happy with him. But then my mother's influence came racing back, and my "sensible" side would take over and realize that I needed to work out my marriage issues first. I was so morally bankrupt at that point. I felt like a fish on dry land, flip-flopping in all directions and not taking a stand for what I wanted or what was truly right.

In 2001, Glen and I decided that maybe moving to a warm climate would help him. We took a trip to New Mexico and fell in love with several areas there. We decided to look for a home in the Albuquerque area. We figured they had a lot of medical facilities nearby, and the climate was so much nicer than the five months of winter that we usually have in Minnesota. Glen made several trips out to New Mexico to look for houses (of course I had to work). Glen put an offer in on a small acreage in the Edgewood area east of Albuquerque. I convinced my girlfriend Valerie to fly out to New Mexico with me so we could see the house and have a short vacation.

I loved the house in Edgewood but was having difficulty seeing how we could convert some of the space for his dad and brother. You see, Glen was unwilling to move unless we could bring both his dad and brother along to live with us. I decided to put my trust in God, and if this home was the right move for us, then so be it. I flew back to Minnesota and set about getting the hobby farm in condition to sell. I got back to Minnesota the first part of September 2001. And then 9/11 happened. It sent the whole country reeling. We still planned to move but were unable to get anyone to come and look at our house. People were staying put until things settled down. We had to let the property in New Mexico go because we couldn't get anyone to buy our hobby farm.

I had resigned myself to the fact that it might take a couple of years for the economy to come back after such a tragic event as 9/11. So I soldiered on going to work, getting together with friends and trying to have dinner once in a while with Tom. By this time, he had divorced his second wife and was sharing custody of their little boy. He still wanted me to divorce Glen and marry him, but again, I just couldn't say yes. He showered me with love and attention at a time when I truly needed it. Glen was still wrapped up in trying to cope with being addicted to prescription painkillers, but I just couldn't pull the trigger and end the marriage. Yet the dogs were always there for me to cuddle with when I came home from work every night. They were always willing to lie down with me and snuggle up to try and keep my emotions on an even keel.

In the spring of 2002, our twenty-fifth anniversary was fast approaching. Glen and I had decided to meet for dinner in Chaska, which was midway between the hobby farm and my workplace in Minneapolis. However, right before I left work to go meet him, he called to say that he couldn't meet for dinner and was home already after taking a new medication that the pain clinic had prescribed. He said it made him feel so spacey and he didn't feel able to drive. He didn't suggest we get together another day. Nope, it was all about him and his pain and how the medication made him feel. I got home that night feeling hurt and rejected, so after feeding and watering the horses, I went upstairs to bed and took a couple of the dogs with me to snuggle. Their calm, steady, loving presence helped to ease the pain and hurt I was feeling.

We made it through 2002 but just barely. Glen had slipped on the ice that winter and hurt himself, and he wanted to move more than ever. I started looking online at northern Arizona. An earthship (a house made out of tires and mudded over) was listed for sale in the town of Kingman. We decided to fly out and see what it was all about.

Kingman is located about ninety miles south of Las Vegas. It's a town of about twenty-five thousand people and is situated on old Route 66 and, more conveniently, right off Interstate 40. We drove out to see the earthship, which was located about ten miles outside of Kingman proper. It was an interesting building, and we might have gone for it if we hadn't had to accommodate Glen's dad and brother. While in Kingman though, we decided to see what homes were for sale. We found a beautiful southwestern ranch-style home on five acres. The house had a four-car attached garage that we could convert to an apartment for Glen's dad and brother, and it also had horse facilities. We decided to make an offer, which was accepted.

Back home we put the hobby farm up for sale again. Sales were much better in 2003, and we sold the farm and set closing for November 1, 2003. We had Teddy, Spotty, Tawney, and Sybil, and you would think that, with four dogs in the house and anticipating a move across country, that would be enough. But in late summer of 2003, we decided to get another sheltie puppy. This time we purchased a little bi-black girl we named Brenna. Brenna means "raven-haired maiden," and she was mostly black in color with very little white. Brenna was as cute as a bug. So in November 2003, off we went on our new adventure in Kingman, Arizona, with the five dogs and two horses.

CHAPTER SEVEN

Brenna

I had my Peruvian Paso horses while living on the hobby farm in Minnesota. These horses have some of the sweetest temperaments in the horse world, and their smooth gait allows people to ride who would not be able to handle the bouncing that goes along with a trotting horse. I kept thinking how great Peruvian Pasos would be for doing equine riding for the handicapped. However, when I checked into possibly doing it on the hobby farm, I found that the liability insurance was too prohibitive for my financial situation at that time.

Feeling a little frustrated that I couldn't help people with disabilities with my beautiful horses, I started looking at how I could possibly use my dogs to help people. After doing several internet searches, I found information on therapy dog work. Up to that point, I had never been clear on the differences between a service dog and a therapy dog. As mentioned before in the book, service dogs are trained by specialized trainers to help one individual try to live life to the fullest whether it be a Seeing Eye dog, a dog that can sense a seizure or PTSD episode coming on or do tasks such as turn on light switches and pick up keys. The recipient of a service dog forms a very deep and special attachment to their service dog. Therapy dogs are owned and trained by everyday people. These dogs are the 'family' dog and live with their family. Therapy dogs need basic obedience training, including heeling on a loose leash, sitting, keeping down, staying, and coming when called. All these training tidbits are necessary, but the fact is that therapy dogs are born, not trained. So what do I mean by that? Let me tell you about training Brenna, my little bi-black sheltie.

Once we arrived and settled down in Kingman, I started searching for a training facility to get Brenna trained on basic obedience. The local feed store offered classes, so off I went to training with Brenna. I sat next to a woman who was training her labradoodle, Doodle. Honestly, I had never seen a labradoodle before, but Doodle was one intelligent and good-looking dog. His owner, Kit, and I started talking and found we both were interested in doing therapy work with our dogs. We religiously trained with our dogs and walked them every day, performing loose leash healing, sitting, and stays. We passed the obedience class with flying colors. Now we needed to find someone to train us on doing therapy dog work.

That training came with the addition of Laura, a local woman who breeds and shows Bernese Mountain Dogs. She wanted to train Tracker, her handsome stud dog, to do therapy work. So the three of us started training by doing the tasks needed to pass the therapy dog test as given by the registering organization Delta (now called Pet Partners). Their test required us to meet and greet a stranger with another dog while our dog sits quietly at our side; walking through a crowd of people with many people reaching and touching the dog; being able to handle all sorts of medical equipment, including wheelchairs, walkers, canes, IV poles, among others; and allowing someone to completely hug the dog by putting their arms totally around the dog.

We had a small group of people who were interested in testing their dogs for therapy work. We practiced several nights a week, often going to shopping areas and walking the dogs past crowds of people pushing grocery carts, or automatic doors opening and closing, walking them up and down stairs, inside and out. We tried to expose the dogs to all sorts of situations and noises so that, if they were in a hospital setting, they wouldn't be alarmed by carts being pushed down aisles or nurses or doctors racing to a room or patients moving with awkward motions. Through all these training maneuvers,

Brenna was able to handle it all. But when it became time to make a visit with a person, she would do it, but her heart was not in it.

As our training progressed, she could handle all the noises, commotion, and obedience tasks without batting an eye. And she would make a visit to people, but only because I asked her to do so. She did not seek out people to be petted; she preferred only my husband or me to give her pets.

So after all the training, I decided to pull her from the program. I was heartbroken, but I honestly felt I couldn't force her to do something she really didn't want to do just because I wanted to do it. And that's why I said earlier that therapy dogs are born, not trained. You can teach any dog to do basic obedience commands, but to do therapy work, you have to have a dog that wants and asks for interaction with people outside their own family. It was a painful lesson to learn, but learn it I did. For years, whenever Laura and Kit trained a new class of possible therapy team recruits, they mentioned Brenna and how important it was to make sure that the dog actually wants to interact with humans. It truly is a fact—therapy dogs are born, not trained.

CHAPTER EIGHT

Casey Mac

After moving to Kingman, we set about converting the four-car attached garage into an apartment for my father-in-law and brother-in-law. We used what was the maid's bedroom and bathroom in that wing of the house for my brother-in-law and then finished off the conversion of the garage into a living room with kitchenette, roll-in shower facility, and big porch doors to roll outside and enjoy the beautiful Arizona weather. You see, my father-in-law was a paraplegic in a wheelchair with a catheter and colostomy bag, and my brother-in-law was schizophrenic and honestly didn't care much for women. By November of 2004, the apartment was ready, so Glen's dad and brother made the trek down to Arizona.

This was my life in Arizona. My father-in-law and brother-in-law were wonderful people, but dealing with three people with serious physical and/or mental issues began to take its toll on me. The agreement was that, since I had worked full-time since we were married, it was now Glen's turn to work full-time and I could work part-time if I wanted or not.

Getting in-home health care for my in-laws was difficult, and Glen often had to do many of the difficult and mundane tasks of getting his dad to bed or cleaned up. I know, between his drug addiction and trying to act as a caregiver to his father and brother, he was unable and probably unwilling to get a job. I decided that I needed to get out of the house, so I took a job with the Superior Court in Kingman.

My job required a lot of interaction with people at the court. I started out in the Clerk of Court's office and worked my way over to restitution clerk, where I had to pay restitution to victims. When we got in the prison checks, often the restitution payment was under a dollar because of the low prison wages. Needless to say, I didn't always see the better side of humanity working at the court. Often when I got home from work, I would find my father-in-law and brother-in-law in our living room, staring at our TV, which was not turned on. When I asked them why they were in our living room and not watching the TV in their apartment, the answer was "We're waiting for Glen to come back from his walk and turn on the TV. We like your TV better."

I probably should let you know that I'm a very private person. Since we never had kids, we didn't have their friends coming over to the house or much activity in and out of the house. Both Glen's and my family are small so we never had relatives stopping over either. Because of this, I grew to enjoy my privacy more and more as I got older. Often when I came home from working at the court, I just needed to decompress for a half hour or so, and I would do that by lying on the bed, closing my eyes, and trying to meditate and relax. However, whenever my in-laws would invite themselves over without Glen there to occupy them, I felt like I had to fill in. Between the pressure-packed court job, a drug-addicted husband, and in-laws who were difficult to care for and keep happy, I found myself edging closer and closer to what I felt to be a mental breakdown. The only things that kept me going and on a somewhat-even keel were my Peruvian Paso horses and my dogs.

There was many a night when I would get home from work, saddle up one of the horses, and ride by myself up into the mountains to clear my head. The dogs too were always there for me to lean on and cuddle. All this was happening at the same time that I was training Brenna, and it hammered home to me how lifesaving these precious animals are.

I still felt so adrift at this time in my life, and because I was feeling the loss of my privacy, the pain of never being able to have children and a crumbling relationship with my husband, I started looking for another dog to enter my life. This was in early 2005. I poured over the listings on Puppyfind.com and found a cute little sable-headed white sheltie puppy. We decided to purchase him, and we had him flown to Las Vegas, where we picked him up one rainy evening.

Casey MacDuff was such a cute pup. He had a beautiful sable-colored head and a predominately-white body with a few sable markings splashed throughout his white coat. He was such a great diversion for me, and I loved this little boy instantly. I couldn't wait to get him started on training.

In the summer of 2005, I started training him with Kit and Laura. Casey was somewhat intelligent and wasn't as shy as some shelties can be. However, Casey had one bad habit that I couldn't train out of him. For some reason, every so often he would just take off and attack whatever dog or object that was near him. I didn't know what was causing this—oversensitive hearing, bad eyes, scrambled brain? I just couldn't figure it out, but here again, Casey was not a born therapy dog, so between the experiences with both Brenna and Casey, this little fact became more and more apparent to me. I finished up with Casey's obedience training but didn't even bother starting him on therapy dog training. There was no way I would ever trust him as a therapy dog since I couldn't predict what situation or circumstances would set him off.

My father-in-law passed away the fall of 2005, and just two weeks before his death, we were able to get my brother-in-law placed in a wonderful group home that worked with schizophrenic patients. I knew this was a difficult time for Glen, and there were many times I saw him cuddling the dogs, trying to overcome his grief.

My affair with Tom also continued during this time. If Glen or I wanted to travel back to Minnesota, we had to do it separately. One of us had to be in Kingman to take care of the dogs and the horses. But whenever I travelled back to Minnesota to visit family, my affair and I made plans to see each other. However, the last time I saw him was Christmas of 2005. He brought take-out dinner over to my hotel room, and we enjoyed our dinner and each other. By the end of the evening though, he couldn't get out of the room fast enough. I was so confused because I was so unhappy at home and wanted to talk about the possibility of getting divorced and moving back to Minnesota, but he was unable to hear me. Whenever I started talking about how bad things were at home, he changed the subject. My heart was breaking. I know I did a terrible thing stringing him along for so many years, whispering that maybe I would get divorced and we could marry. But obviously he had had enough of being the other man.

Christmas with my family found me smiling and acting happy in front of my family. But inside I was so broken—both my heart and my spirit. And then I had to go home and face an addicted husband, who refused to believe that maybe the opioid painkillers he had been taking for five years were doing damage to his brain. As I flew back home to Arizona, the only thing that brought any joy to me was the fact I would be seeing my dogs and horses in a few hours. I couldn't wait to saddle up one of the horses and ride into the mountains and just let my thoughts wander. I had a lot of thinking I needed to do—should I end my marriage? Should I try to patch it up with my affair? How would I survive financially getting divorced? How would we ever split up the dogs in a fair and equitable manner? As 2006 dawned, I hadn't made any decisions yet on what direction I wanted my life to go. Instead I settled into the same old routine of going to work every day and coming home to a totally dysfunctional marriage. Something had to change!

CHAPTER NINE

Mario

We had six dogs living in Arizona—Sybil, Tawney, Spotty, Teddy, Brenna, and Casey. Those six were definitely a handful, but they each were wonderful dogs in their own way. However, I still felt sad that I didn't have a dog that could do therapy work with me. Tawney, the collie, was getting too old. Sybil was pretty much too ornery, and Teddy and Spotty were friendly shelties but honestly didn't seek out affection from other people outside the family as is often the case with shelties. Brenna had definitely shown me that she had no interest in interacting with strangers outside the family, and Casey was not therapy dog material. But until another potential therapy dog came along, I continued doing what I always do—go to work and come home and be unhappy.

On my birthday in 2006, I discovered that Glen had been having an affair with a former girlfriend. The reality of the situation was a surprise, but then again not a surprise. For years, neither of us had taken the time to nurture our relationship, and the fruits of that lack of caring and nurturing resulted in both of us having an affair. I'm not going to lie—I was hurt, but how could I get angry at him when I myself had had an affair lasting nineteen years? It would be like the pot calling the kettle black.

The gravity of my marital situation weighed heavily on me, and I couldn't believe how low I had sunk. I spent many nights sitting outside on the back porch, crying and hugging my faithful, furry companions, who followed me outside. I railed against God for letting my life become such an empty pit. And that's exactly how I felt—empty, broken, childless, and worthless. But in all my nighttime outside musings, I realized my life was in the place it was because of decisions I had made. Glen and I had equally squandered our marriage for greener pastures. During the tumultuous summer of 2006, I was glad that I didn't have children, because I knew any children would have been hurt and confused over this marriage, which was in a shambles. This would have been the perfect time for me to spill the beans about my affair and to end the marriage at that point and go our separate ways. But that's not what happened.

I still went to work every day and put on this false face of happiness. But then I would come home, feed the horses, and retreat into the master bedroom with a couple of the dogs and watch TV. I can't believe how numb I was back then. Every night I mulled over my options—stay in a loveless marriage? Demand a divorce? Move back to Minnesota? I was in such a quandary over what to do. So I just kept going to work and becoming even more depressed.

I firmly believe that God places people and animals in our lives at just the right time. One Friday in July 2006, I was on my way to work when I made the decision to stop and buy the local paper, along with something for lunch. Honestly, I had never picked up the paper before, but for some reason, I felt compelled to do so on that day. While eating my lunch, I perused the paper and came to the page where they listed animals available for adoption at the local shelter. Right smack dab in the middle was a picture of a sable-and-white sheltie that they had named Mario, who was going to be available for adoption when the shelter opened the next morning. What can I say—I was there at ten o'clock when the shelter opened and looked at this sad-looking sheltie in a wire cage in a metal building with no air moving through. I didn't even think twice, opened up my wallet and handed them the money for Mario.

I got the scoop on Mario from the shelter personnel as they knew it. He had been picked up as a stray, was covered with feces when he was taken into the shelter, but seemed very friendly. He had come right up to me in his cage and nosed me through the wires. He sat like a little gentleman on the three-mile ride to his new home.

Mario was adorable. He was a rich, deep shade of sable with a full white collar and a huge white strip on his nose that reached around both eyes to his chin. Mar was pretty overweight, so at least I knew he hadn't been starved. He also seemed to take the current pack at home in stride and didn't force himself on any of the other dogs. Mario was a very laid-back little boy who loved just about everyone he met. I already loved him immensely for I had finally found a dog I could train to do therapy work. I couldn't wait to call Kit and have her meet my new little boy! Of course, Glen wasn't happy that I had brought home another dog, but I didn't care what he thought. I only knew I needed to give this dog a home and together maybe we could work on becoming a therapy team and maybe I could find some self-respect and redemption once I became a therapy team.

Kingman is located in the northwest section of Arizona. There are no close large towns nearby, and trying to find a Delta evaluator or tester to come and test our dogs in Kingman was becoming a tough project. Delta (now called Pet Partners) is one of the national registering organizations for therapy dog teams. Because Kit and Laura had not found an evaluator yet, they were still training in therapy work, so I seized the opportunity to train Mario.

Mario passed his obedience training in no time, and then we went to work on getting him used to hospital equipment, noises, going up and down stairs, handling a crowd of people, and being steady and calm around other dogs. Mario was handling the training like a pro. He looked forward to our walks every day and faithfully did whatever I asked of him. Mario was an all-star!

In the fall of 2006, my crumbling marriage relationship was too unbearable for me to live with Glen in Arizona anymore. There were so many mistakes made by both of us and so many things left unsaid. I made the decision to move back to Minnesota with Mario to be near my family so maybe I could heal and gain some self-respect. I rented a house about a mile from my father and just three miles from my mother, who was in a facility, called Rahkma House, for those suffering with Alzheimer's. Dad loved driving over to my house and seeing Mario. He had a cat at that time that he loved immensely, but he truly was a dog person, and I could see how his face would light up whenever Mario jumped up next to him on the couch and Dad would eagerly pet him. I could tell therapy work was going to be such a rewarding experience not only for the recipient of the dog's affection but for me too.

Before I had moved back to Minnesota, Tawney, my sweet collie, had been showing signs of slowing down. She was approaching twelve years old, which nowadays is considered old age for bigger dogs. But she also started to lose weight, and I was afraid that maybe she had cancer. I wanted to bring her with me back to Minnesota, but the owners of the house I was renting in Minnesota would only allow one small dog in the rental house.

In November of 2006, Tawney's back legs gave out. Glen had to call my friend Kit to help him carry Tawney on a makeshift stretcher so he could take her into the vet's office. Sadly, she had to be put down at that visit. I felt so guilty that I wasn't with her when she passed over. I can only pray that she knew how much I loved her and how her gentle nature and love of people influenced me so that I will always have collies in my life.

In January of 2007, Glen decided to admit himself into rehab and get off the pain medication. It was a brave move for him, and I knew that he had many months of therapy ahead. I decided to move back to Kingman to help him get through the group therapy appointments. So back to Kingman Mario and I went. Around the same time, Kit and Laura had found an evaluator in Prescott, Arizona, who was willing to evaluate our dogs for Delta if we came down there. So off went six of us with our dogs to be evaluated. I was really nervous to be tested—much more nervous than Mario, and here's my reason. Mario is a food-oriented dog. When he did things correctly, he got a treat. However, you are not allowed to give your dog treats while being tested, and I was afraid that, after a few commands that he performed and didn't receive a treat for his efforts, that would cause him to not comply the next time I asked him to do something. But Mar came through like a trooper. The only part he didn't do well was when they hooked him to an eighteen-foot leash (it was actually a horse lunge line). He didn't want to come because he didn't like the weight of dragging that long line. I can't say I blamed him. They marked him off for it, but it wasn't enough that we didn't pass the test. What a feeling—after trying to train Brenna and Casey and the resulting disappointment of pulling them from the program and then on a fluke, finding Mario at a shelter and training intensely with him for nine months—victory was never so sweet! Now Mario and I could start making therapy visits.

Three times a week, I attended group therapy sessions with Glen. I was so haughty at our first visit. When the facilitator asked me questions, I put all the blame on Glen and his addiction to the pain medication. Man, did that facilitator give me a verbal smack on the head when she said no one she knew would have put up with the crap that Glen had given me the past seven years. Whoa, that smarts. By the end of the eight weeks of group therapy sessions, I was told I was codependent and should attend a group in the Kingman area to overcome codependency.

I'm all for improving myself, so I attended a meeting of the codependency group in Kingman. We went around the room and gave our name and the reasons we felt we were codependent creatures. I gave my spiel, and then the baton was passed to the woman seated next to me. Her story was very heartfelt, and she talked about how she had become addicted to gambling, living with an abusive husband, lost her kids, and had spent all her retirement money on gambling. This woman was sobbing as she related losing custody of her children. There was a box of Kleenex sitting on the table, and I grabbed one and handed it to her. Oh my god, you would think I had just shot someone. The facilitator chewed my hind end for giving this woman a Kleenex. I was keeping her codependent—if she wanted a Kleenex, she could get it or ask for it. While I understand the philosophy behind it, I don't want to be part of any group where performing a simple act of kindness to a fellow human being causes the group to have mass hysteria. So I quit right on the spot.

When Glen and I had started the group therapy together, he had agreed that he would stop talking to his "girlfriend" and work on our relationship. But that didn't happen. Our thirtieth anniversary rolled around that April, and I wanted to celebrate by going to Hawaii. We had been to Hawaii a couple of times before, and I found it to be so beautiful and romantic there. I honestly felt we deserved (or maybe I should say I deserved) a good anniversary celebration, considering how our twenty-fifth anniversary celebration was nonexistent. But Glen had no interest in going anywhere. He only wanted to drive up to Vegas for dinner. It was obvious that he was still in touch with his affair. Since anything resembling working on our marriage seemed to be nonexistent, I decided to throw myself into the therapy work with Mario.

After both Kit and I passed the Delta evaluation test, we wanted to start making visits at the Kingman Regional Hospital. Kit got in contact with the volunteer coordinator, and we scheduled a date for our first visit. But before we could make any visits, we had to go through "volunteer training" at the hospital. This included learning what different warning signals were in force and what to do should any of these signals be broadcast. We also learned that we had to stay away from any room with a red card on the door. The red cards indicated a patient who had a contagious disease or infection such as MRSA. MRSA, the bacterial infection that was difficult to treat, was beginning to rear its ugly head. We also had to get a tuberculosis (TB) test, update records on our previous immunizations, and have a picture ID taken with our dogs. After a couple of weeks of training, we humans were ready to start visiting.

The training period for our dogs continued after we started actual visits. First we had to train the dogs to be able to handle being in an elevator and adjusting to the elevator's movements. Then we had to get them used to walking on highly polished linoleum floors—something some of the dogs were not comfortable with as they couldn't get much traction for walking on the slick floors. Then we made sure they were comfortable going up or down the stairwells in case of an emergency when the elevators were not to be used. Also, we walked the dogs around the crowded halls filled with hospital personnel, crash carts, medicine carts, etc. Once we felt assured that the dogs were comfortable in different situations, then we started making visits.

Kit and I tried to make visits at the hospital at least three times a week. We had some wonderful visits with patients who were so grateful to be able to pet a dog and get some comfort. We also had some visits with people who were not necessarily of sound mind and would be almost too rough on the dogs. In situations like those, it is important for the handler to remove the dog from any situation where the dog's welfare and safety are in question. I feel I am the advocate for my dog on the visits. My main goal of course is to bring "therapy" to the people we visit, but first and foremost, I want my dog to have a positive experience also. There were a couple of times when I had to cut the visit short because the patient was getting a little too aggressive in petting Mario. Mario is fairly chubby (a problem with a lot of shelties as they get older), and people really do love to sink their fingers into his soft fur and rub. And while some dogs can handle being petted with a firm hand, Mario is much more sensitive and will display his discomfort by growling under his breath.

Things went well visiting two or three days a week at the Kingman Regional Hospital. One day when Kit and I went in to start making visits, hospital volunteers were tasked with taking the blood pressure readings of all visitors entering the facility. Many of the visitors had high blood pressure readings, and in some cases, these high readings may have been the result of worrying about family and friends in the hospital. This went on for a while when Kit suggested changing up the procedure. First the volunteer would take the person's blood pressure and then bring in one of the therapy dogs and take a second reading while allowing the person to pet the dog at the same time. We were shocked at the results. Everyone had at least a ten-point drop in their blood pressure. Now I know this was not a scientific study under controlled circumstances, so it would have been discounted by the scientific community. But for me, this was just more positive proof of the influence of dogs and how they truly can help us heal.

Before making any visit, Delta's rules required us to give our dog a bath. Mario hated baths. The minute he saw me coming with towels and dog shampoo, he would hightail it out of the bathroom and hide. Honestly, it was a struggle to give him a bath every time, so I ended up getting a product that was a waterless bath for dogs. Mario still didn't like it, but he tolerated the waterless bath much more than a regular bath.

I remember being so cautious about not entering any room with a red crash cart next to it and a red card on the door. MRSA was starting its insidious advance on people, and the current antibiotics were not up to the task of keeping it at bay at that time. I remember one incident when one of the therapy teams that had taken the test along with Kit and me had gone into a patient room. The room did not have a red crash cart or red card on the door. Virginia went into the room and started up a conversation with the patient, who was more than happy to have Coco come and visit. Virginia lifted Coco on the bed next to the patient so he could pet and cuddle him. As they were talking, the patient indicated that he was in the hospital because he had a "raging MRSA infection." Virginia turned white at the mention of MRSA and quickly ended the conversation and took Coco out of the room. She raced over to where Kit and I were visiting and explained what had happened. She was in a panic, fearing that maybe both she and Coco would contract a MRSA infection. We had her leave immediately, go home, and give Coco a bath and herself a long hot shower and told her to wash her clothes in hot water. Then we went to the nursing station on that floor and told them what had happened and that they needed to correct the problem as soon as possible so that others would not become accidentally contaminated. To this day, I don't know if those were the correct instructions to give Virginia, but neither she nor Coco ever developed MRSA.

Kit is a wonderful PR person, and she contacted several teachers at the local elementary school to see if they were interested in having the dogs come in to the classroom and let the kids read to the dogs. Dogs are nonjudgmental, and the READ© program based out of Colorado has proven that children having difficulty reading do so much better reading to the dogs than reading in front of their peers. The dogs sit there patiently while the child reads to them, and the handler asks the child questions regarding the story they are reading to make sure they comprehend what they are reading. It's a great program, and we were given the go-ahead to start making visits to the second-grade class.

Kit and I decided to add some challenges to our visit by coming up with some simple math problems for the kids to solve that were dog based. For instance, one of the questions was "If Doodle's tail is eighteen inches long and Mario's tail is twelve inches long, how long would they be if you laid them end to end?" The kids loved the questions because they could visualize putting the tails end to end with the dogs sitting right in front of them.

Kit and I visited once a week in the school and sometimes as often as three times a week at the hospital. All along I was getting better at making visits and striking up conversations with people. I often felt that our visits to the hospital were more for giving the staff a break from their tough jobs than visiting patients. Whenever Kit, Doodle, Mario, and I would appear in the hallway, we would hear a chorus of "The dogs are here, the dogs are here," and nurses and even doctors would come over to pet the dogs and take five minutes to decompress from their difficult jobs.

Again because Kit was so good at public relations regarding the dogs, she got approval from the administrator that we could take our dogs into the hospital cafeteria and grab a bite to eat when we were making visits. Whenever we would sit at a table in the cafeteria, doctors, nurses, and even visitors would come over to the table and pet the dogs and ask us a lot of questions about the dogs and what therapy dogs do. All during this time of making visits, sitting in the cafeteria, talking about our dogs and even visiting the schools, I realized that I personally was getting more out of these visits than those that we were visiting did.

Such was my life during the year 2007. My marriage was still in shambles, but I was slowly learning to like myself again because of the therapy visits we were making. My self-respect started to rise from the depths of despair, and my nighttime outdoor crying jags stopped all together. Glen had decided that we should sell the house in Kingman and move back to Minnesota. I really did miss my family, and I wanted to spend as much time with my parents as I could before they passed away. But I truly enjoyed those days of visiting patients and seeing the smiles on people's faces as they caressed Mario, ran their fingers through his soft fur, and were able to ask questions about the therapy dogs, thus allowing them to forget for a few minutes the various reasons they were in the hospital in the first place. But as with all good things, the time came when we sold our house and moved back to Minnesota. On to the next phase of my life.

CHAPTER TEN

Harley

In the late fall of 2007, we made the move back to Minnesota. We were living in a small town (fifteen thousand residents) outside the Twin Cities, and I hadn't made any therapy team contacts yet since moving back. Delta's website had a listing of registered teams sorted by state. At that time, there were a few teams in the same county as I was, and since I much prefer visiting with other teams, I contacted them via email and asked if they might like to try making some visits together. I never got any responses back. Maybe these teams had always made visits on their own and weren't familiar with how much more fun it was to visit with other teams. But no matter, I sought out assisted living residences and the local nursing home as places that Mario and I could visit.

Off Mario and I went to the local nursing home. I don't think they had ever had therapy dog teams visit before, as they seemed somewhat confused as to what they should do and expect from Mario and me. I told them to just point me in the direction of residents who might like to have a visit from a dog. They did just that, and Mario and I were off and running.

Teddybear developed an abscessed tooth. His poor face and mouth were all swollen on one side. We hadn't made any vet contacts yet, so we pulled out the phone book and called the nearest vet. They told us to take him in and they would do surgery that day. In the middle of the afternoon, we got a call from the vet's office. Teddy had died on the table in surgery. I was in shock. How could that be? He was fine when we took him in for the surgery. Unfortunately, this was another nail in the coffin of my marriage. Glen and I had had so many deaths, illnesses, and loss that, instead of helping each other through the hard times, each new loss drove the wedge deeper into our relationship. To deal with the grief, I threw myself into making as many visits with Mario as I could.

Throughout the spring and summer of 2008, I made several visits each month to the nursing home and to one of the assisted-living centers designed for people with disabilities. Mario and I really enjoyed visiting there, and we made quite a few friends. We lost some of our nursing home residents, but I knew they had passed on to the next phase of their soul's lives.

Throughout the winter and spring of 2008, my mom's Alzheimer's was progressing. I had taken Mario to visit her one day. I knew she didn't recognize me (and that always hurt even though I knew she couldn't help it), but I figured Mario might stir some memory in her of Tammy, Brandy, and Tanya. Nope, she had no interest in petting Mario but instead preferred one of the caregiver's dogs. This caregiver took her beautiful golden retriever with her every day to work as she knew animals had the ability to break through to Alzheimer's patients. Mom loved the golden retriever but could have cared less about interacting with Mario. Oh well, so much for that idea.

In August of 2008, Mom fell at the care facility and broke her hip. We declined to have her go through the surgery because she would not be able to comply with rehab. We chose comfort care for her and wanted her to be free of pain. She was placed in hospice and died ten days after entering the hospice facility. The same week that my mom passed away, Glen and I filed for divorce. There was no animosity in our breakup. There was only a reality that we had both made so many bad decisions throughout our marriage that it was unsalvageable. We were able to finalize the divorce after four weeks. I needed to find a place to live and found a wonderful 1924 brick four-square close to the downtown area. After some repairs and upgrades to the house, I moved in at the end of October. Well, actually, Mario, Sybil, and I moved in to our new house.

The past three years had been so traumatic for me—moving back to Minnesota, dealing with Glen's addiction and going through group therapy, the end of my affair without having closure on the relationship, Mom dying, getting divorced, and having to find and move into my own place. I felt like all these events kept rolling over me like a wave, and like water in a wave, I felt I couldn't grasp onto anything and make a firm decision about the direction of my life. I had lived at home with my parents until I got married. But here I was at fifty-four, alone for the first time in my life. It was totally scary to me. But I did as my parents had taught me all those years ago: "Suck it up, buttercup. Raise your head and carry on in the best way you know how."

I wasn't working at that time, so I decided to go back to school and complete my bachelor's degree. I had enough credits from going to the University of Minnesota to be considered in my mid–junior year, so I decided to go for a degree in natural health and to complete my degree by taking an online course of study. My mom had really placed a high value on education, and I always felt bad that I had never finished my degree. So for a year and a half, my days were filled with working toward my degree.

During that same time, I noticed that Sybil was not very happy living with Mario. She truly missed her puppies Teddy and Spotty, so Glen took Sybil back to his house to live. When I adopted Mario, the vet thought he was between five and eight years old. He had already been with me for two years, so I became somewhat worried that Mario would only be able to do therapy work for a few more years, and I had decided that making therapy visits with my dogs was something that I wanted to do for the rest of my life. So I decided to purchase a puppy that I could train to do therapy work and therefore have a pick of dogs to make visits with in case one of them was ill or having an off day.

In the fall of 2008, I started perusing the Puppyfind website and the local Minnesota Sheltie Rescue and Minnesota Wisconsin Collie Rescue websites for adoptable dogs. While both of the rescue sites had wonderful dogs for adoption, I came back to that truism that therapy dogs are born, not trained. Many of the adoptable dogs have trauma in their backgrounds—some of the trauma can be overcome, and some can't. I decided to go for a collie puppy, a color-headed white collie puppy, in particular. I knew that such a rare color of collie would be an icebreaker on therapy visits, and people to this day comment on Harley's beautiful and rare coloring. I found just the puppy I was looking for on the Puppyfind website. He was a blue-merle-headed white collie. His body was all white with no color spots on it, and he was adorable.

I quickly purchased him and had him flown out here from Kentucky where he was from the week before Thanksgiving of 2008. Flying a dog was a totally new experience for me. Harley made the trip on Northwest Airlines (now Delta), and his crate was taken to the cargo building on the Minneapolis/St. Paul airport grounds. I had to show proof of purchase for Harley, which I did, and quickly took him out to my car. I swear he was the most handsome puppy I had ever seen. His whole body was snowy white in color with a beautifully shaped collie head of grayish-blue merle coloring and gorgeous almond-shaped tawny-colored eyes. He was absolutely adorable, and I rushed off to show him to Dad, who lived only a few miles from the airport. Dad enjoyed holding Harley and thought he was really cute, but it was time for me to take Harley home to see how he and Mario would get along.

Thanksgiving and Christmas of 2008 were very emotionally draining for me. I found myself crying myself to sleep many nights. I felt numb for many months. I had even contemplated ending my life. I was so overcome with grief at the loss of my mom and my marriage so close together. But having the dogs there really kept me focused and grounded. Having the dogs meant that I had to get up every morning to let them out and feed them and repeat the procedure every evening. Getting Harley was the best thing I could have done. He brought new life into the household with his funny puppy maneuvers and dizzying runs through the house. Yup, I had to be there to care for the dogs, let them out, feed them, nurture them, and train them. At that point, they became the children I was never able to have.

So I spent the year 2009 studying to complete my degree, training Harley, and making therapy visits with Mario. I finally felt that I had some purpose to my life. Previous to that, I felt like I had been stumbling through life. After I dropped out of college in the 1970s, I went to the Minnesota School of Business to become a court reporter. It was work I found interesting, and I passed the exam and became a certified court reporter a year after I married. However, the only jobs available at that time were in Peoria, Illinois, and Brookings, South Dakota. My husband and I had purchased a house in Farmington, Minnesota, by then, so Peoria was not an option. I applied for the Brookings, South Dakota, job, but it was a traveling court with a male judge, and he didn't feel it was appropriate for a male judge to travel with a female court reporter. You have to remember this was 1978 and things were different back then. So I took a job as a secretary at a life insurance agency and then moved over as a secretary to the CFO of Sperry Univac, a job my father-in-law helped me get.

I had been working for Dave at Sperry Univac for a year when he asked me if I wanted to try my hand in the Accounts Receivable department. He felt I was being wasted as a secretary as he could see that I was good with numbers. Off I went to the Accounts Receivable area, where I worked for several years before moving to Cost of Sales and then to a different division, Technical Services Division, where I did all sorts of accounting-related things. Eventually, in 1989 I got laid off from Univac (In 1989 it was called Unisys after Burroughs and Sperry combined).

Three months after getting laid off, I got a job as the office manager for a dental clinic in Minneapolis. This was a great job with a wonderful group of people. Everyone in the clinic had many years of service, and that longevity told me that it truly was a family of people working there, and everyone really cared about one another outside the clinic. I worked there for almost fifteen years until the move to Arizona.

While I enjoyed my years working at the dental clinic, I still felt that I wasn't doing or accomplishing what I was put here on earth to do. And what that specific task or tasks was, I had no clue at that point. But I felt that, up to that point in 2008 and 2009, I had been floating through life, not really taking charge of my life and choosing what I wanted and needed to accomplish. It felt like life was passing me by and I hadn't taken advantage of opportunities to reach out and grab for my dreams. And I also felt that I had made many bad decisions throughout my life that didn't lead me to happiness. I truly wanted to find peace in my life, earn my own way, stand on my own two feet, and figure out how I could possibly give back to people instead of taking all the time. I had this feeling running through my head that somehow the therapy dogs would be part of my life's purpose.

So in spring of 2009, I worked at training Harley at home and making visits with Mario. Mario was registered with Delta, and Delta requires their therapy teams to take the test every two years, so I started looking for a place where I could take the test. I searched through Delta's website for upcoming tests in the Twin Cities area and found a place in South Minneapolis where I could take the test. We drove over one evening to take the test. While we were waiting for our turn, a couple was taking the test together with their two collies. The collies "talked" throughout the whole test, and I was surprised by that. Do any of you remember the TV show *Lassie*? When Lassie tried to tell people that Timmy fell in the well, she didn't bark, but made sounds almost like a whine. That's what these two dogs were doing throughout the test. I was amazed that this couple had passed the test because of their "talking" dogs. Little did I know that talking collies would be a major thing in my life. Mario and I passed the test, so we set out for home feeling pretty good about ourselves. I even bought Mario a victory ice-cream cone on the way home.

All the therapy-dog-registering organizations require that the dog be at least one year of age before being tested. That meant that I couldn't test Harley until at least the fall of 2009. Being a collie, Harley had a propensity to jump up on people in his zeal to greet them and have people pet him. However, jumping up on people is a huge fault when doing therapy dog work. Our training continued on way past the date that I could test him in 2009 because of his jumping up on people. Also, during all our obedience classes, Harley liked to "talk." It wasn't a bark, but a high-pitched sound that came out his mouth. Most of the talking is because he is so excited to see people and he wants them to notice him and how handsome he is. I was mortified in class because Harley didn't seem able to shut up. Our trainer at EZ Obedience, Char Gatz, told me to relax and said that every collie she had worked with previously did some form of talking. I don't know if collies talk because they are trying to emulate Lassie and tell us Timmy fell in the well. But I do know I don't really appreciate it. It's something that Harley does to this day, and it seems like it's a common fault in collies. I guess they just have so much to say to us.

Because I wasn't willing to test Harley until he settled down somewhat from being such a puppy and jumping up on people, I decided to try making hospice visits with Mario. I drove into Minneapolis to take the training, and after passing the hospice training, we started making hospice visits to patients in the Twin Cities area. While I truly enjoyed doing hospice work, I really didn't like driving so far to make the visits. Mario and I did hospice work in the Twin Cities area for about two years.

At this same time, Mario and I participated in a children's reading program at our local library. He did fine the first couple of weeks, but one evening, one of the youngsters was a bit rough in handling him, and I could feel Mario growling under his breath. Oops, that's a no-no. I immediately removed Mario from the program. The fact that Mario growled less than two months after taking the Delta test proved to me that taking a test every two years is not the true hallmark of a good therapy team. Training responsible handlers and handlers who are advocates for their dogs is the correct answer. My local obedience trainer, Char Gatz, and I had spent some time talking while I was in the process of training Harley. She had gotten some feedback from other students in her obedience classes that there was a real interest in testing for doing therapy work. However, Char was not too keen on testing every two years, and neither was I. So we decided to go with Therapy Dogs International (TDI), and Char found an evaluator who was willing to come out and test all the teams that wanted to take the test. In late fall of 2010, Tim came out to Hutchinson, where I live, and evaluated eight teams. Harley and

I had passed the test, and I was beyond excited to start making visits with Harley.

The teams that passed the TDI test wanted to form a group or a chapter, as TDI calls it. I've always felt that it's more fun making visits with other people. TDI had sent us requests from facilities in the area that wanted therapy dog visits for their residents. We started making visits to the local nursing home, several assisted-living centers in our town and other towns around us, long-term-care facilities, and we had some requests for us to take our dogs into a couple of schools in the area for the children to read to the dogs. We were on a roll, and I was really enjoying making visits with Harley until he opened his mouth to talk. His talking got to be so annoying that I felt I couldn't use him for hospice work because the noise was so totally jarring to people.

The following year, I tested Mario with TDI, and I continued to use Mario doing hospice work because Mario could handle elderly people who didn't make quick movements such as children did. But I knew I would have to retire Mario soon because I really didn't want to take a chance on him biting someone who petted him too roughly. I just didn't feel I could trust him.

I ended up retiring Mario in 2014. For over a year, Mario enjoyed his retirement and his dinners. He was one of the loudest of my dogs to let me know that he was hungry and wanted me to feed him. One Saturday evening in November of 2015, I went out to dinner with a girlfriend. I told her that I had really noticed Mario was slowing down, but I attributed it to arthritis and had started giving him turmeric golden paste every evening with his meal. When I got home from dinner, Mario was sitting in the office, but his body was all askew and his right hind leg was hanging out at an odd angle. I let the dogs out, but Mario could barely walk—wavering and almost dragging his hind legs was more like it. I thought maybe he had had a stroke or a seizure or maybe the other dogs had been roughhousing while I was gone and had run him over in their quest to chase one another. I carried Mario upstairs and laid him on his dog bed, where he immediately went to sleep.

The next day, I called the emergency vet as Mario had no interest in breakfast or in going outside to go potty. She told me to keep watch over him but to take him into the clinic the next day if nothing had improved. Later that afternoon, I offered Mario a piece of prime rib, and he turned his nose at it. This was so not Mario—if he had been feeling well, he would have gobbled up the prime rib and a couple of my fingers in the process. I knew I had to take him in the next day.

Bright and early Mario and I were at the vet's office. They drew blood to run tests and then examined him. Once the bloodwork was in, we knew what was wrong, and it was much worse than a stroke or a seizure. Mario had advanced kidney disease, and his kidneys were shutting down totally. His creatinine level was literally off the chart. Creatinine is a product of muscle metabolism. It is removed from the blood by the kidneys, so a higher level of creatinine may indicate that the kidneys are deficient.

The options for my beautiful boy were very limited: They could hospitalize him, and they could pump fluids into him for five days to see if they could get his kidneys functioning again. They were very skeptical that this would work. Next option was to take him home for a few days to say our goodbyes, and last was to euthanize him then and there. I couldn't stop crying—I had no clue he was in such bad shape. I've always prided myself on feeding my dogs excellently, pulling titers to check for antibodies to various diseases instead of automatically vaccinating them and providing natural herbs and supplements. How did it go from him inhaling his dinner on Saturday evening to being at death's door? Looking at my sweet boy, I couldn't make him suffer any longer—you could see the misery in his eyes. So I chose the only option that I felt was in Mario's best interests—I sent him to the Rainbow Bridge right then and there.

After Mario was gone, I forced myself to go home, clean up, and go to work. The other dogs knew right away when I walked in the door that something had dramatically changed. I made it through work, came home, cooked a good meal for my fur babies, and lay down and cried the whole night.

Ode to Mario: Oh, Mario, I miss you so much. You were the inspiration for me finding my life's purpose—to bring cheer to others through doing therapy work. I am forever grateful to you for giving me nine and a half years of devotion and love and sharing adventures as we visited the elderly and children both. I'm expecting you to be waiting for me at the Rainbow Bridge when it's my time to leave here. Love and miss you, Mario.

Tammy and Me

Brandy as a puppy

Tanya and Brandy

Tanya

Angus

My twin nieces, Julie and Erika, with Angus in between

Heather as a puppy

Heather

Blue as a puppy

Blue meeting Carly for the first time

Tawney as a puppy

Tawney

Sybil as a puppy

Tawney and Sybil playing

Cappy

Spotty, Kirby and Teddy Bear as puppies

Brenna and Spotty

Casey

Mario

Harley

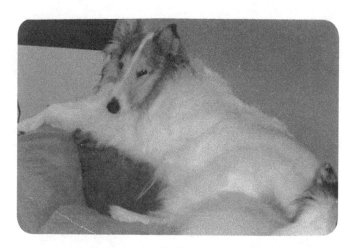

Shelby

Collin

Domino

Skylar on a visit

Olaf

Me with the Dynamic Deaf Duo—Skylar and Olaf

Mackie

CHAPTER ELEVEN

Shelby and Collin

Five years before losing my beloved Mario, I had been perusing various sheltie and collie rescue sites, plus I also like to keep tabs on the Puppyfind website, where I found Harley. In early 2010, I saw an ad on Puppyfind for a coming four-year-old sable-headed white female collie. She came from a breeder in Tennessee who was selling all her stock to move back to Washington. I called the owner, and she told me that the dog was super friendly and would make a great therapy dog. So I decided to buy Shelby, and we agreed to meet in St. Louis, where I would pick her up.

Once I had Shelby home, I started her on beginning obedience classes. She had such a sweet demeanor and really does like people. She will quietly come up to visitors and put her long collie nose in people's hands, asking them to pet her. Shelby on the whole is a couch-potato type of dog. She rarely gets excited, and so I figured she would make a great therapy dog. However, Shelby had one issue that would prevent her from passing the TDI therapy dog test.

Part of the test requires that a loud noise happen—dropping books on the floor or dropping a baby gate are a few examples—and the dog can react but must recover quickly. Whenever Shelby was subjected to the loud noise, she came unglued and shuddered and was visibly upset. I couldn't figure out what was going on with her. She was also extremely fearful whenever we had thunderstorms. So

I called her former owner and asked her about Shelby's issues with loud noises.

The story told to me was that all the breeder's dogs were kept outdoors in kennels. Being they are collies, they bark. Neighbor kids down the road didn't like all the barking, so they threw cherry bombs at the dogs. Now I had the reason Shelby was so fearful of loud noises, and I also knew that I probably would never be able to desensitize her to loud noises. To this day, whenever the fire alarm batteries start chirping, Shelby is in a panic, running in circles and panting heavily. So Shelby has become my sweet girl who prefers to spend her time sleeping on the couch and anticipates every meal. Whenever there is a thunderstorm warning, I have to put a Thundershirt on Shelby. The Thundershirt seems to keep her calmer and provides her comfort during bad storms.

In 2010, I became a member of the Minnesota Wisconsin Collie Rescue and was approved to foster dogs. My first foster, Collin, came to me Memorial weekend of 2010. He was a beautiful sable-and-white collie who had been picked up by a shelter in Wisconsin after running loose for months. While in the shelter, he was given the requisite vaccinations that dogs get, but in Collin's case, it was too much all at once. He developed an autoimmune disorder from being overvaccinated. His autoimmune disorder manifested itself in one of his eyes, and he had an issue with the third eyelid of his right eye. Collin didn't seem bothered by his eye disorder—he seemed to just live with it.

Collin also had a friendly, loving mannerism, and after only two weeks as a foster in my home, I became a "foster flunky" and adopted him. We started obedience training right away, and in spring of 2011, we took the TDI test together and passed. Now I had two dogs that I could visit with since I had not tested Mario with TDI yet.

Collin was such a regal collie. His collie nose was a mile long, but he carried himself with much bravado. He was not at all like Harley in that Harley was always excited and "talking" when visiting people. Collin was much more laid-back and quiet yet willing to come to people for pets of his silky long sable fur.

Harley and Collin both went on therapy visits with me to hospice patients in the area, nursing homes, and assisted-living centers. I noticed with both of my collies that they had issues with different types of flooring. Neither one of them liked walking on linoleum tile or hardwood floors. I couldn't figure out why they were having issues with floors until I realized that they seemed to slip on tile floors and couldn't get a good grip with their paws on the floor. I feel terrible in that, the first time I visited a health-care facility in a neighboring town to visit a hospice patient, Collin wouldn't walk on the linoleum floor, so I literally had to drag him down the corridor to the hospice patient's bedside. After visiting our patient, I decided to see if anyone in the community room area wanted a visit from a therapy dog. Holy Hannah, the first thing Collin did when walking on the carpet in the community room was lift his leg on a piece of furniture.

I was totally embarrassed at my dog's behavior, and I spent the next fifteen minutes cleaning the carpet. I purchased some "paw wax" and used it on Collin when we visited certain facilities that had slippery floors. The paw wax seemed to help although neither collie liked walking on inside surfaces other than carpet. And I made sure to have Collin do his bathroom duties before we entered any facility in the future.

I remember making a hospice visit at our local hospice house first with Collin and on a second visit with Harley. The patient that we were visiting was sitting in a chair, chatting with his brother, who was also there. Harley did everything at this visit he is known for—talking and wanting to jump up on people—or in this case, he put his paws on either side of the patient's lap and stood nose to nose with him, talking the whole time. I was absolutely mortified that Harley was talking so much, but the patient told me he liked talking with Harley and that he had had a collie on his farm for many years—something he had told me on the visit I made with Collin the prior week. After thirty minutes of Harley and the patient talking to each other, we made our exit.

I was saddened to learn of the patient's passing the following week. The family invited me to his funeral, and I decided to go and pay my respects to this really nice man. The brother, who had been visiting him when Harley and I made our visit, commented in his eulogy about his brother and about how much the visit from Harley and me had meant to his brother. He talked about it for days afterward and absolutely loved how he felt that he and Harley had really been talking to each other. So I guess you never know how you will touch people when you're making a visit—even if you're positive your dog is doing the absolute wrong thing!

I stopped doing hospice work in 2013 as I had some issues with the requirements expected of the therapy dog teams. At each visit, I was supposed to fill out a form indicating the patient's emotional state and other observations such as were they in a good mood, bad mood, depressed, etc. The majority of times when I visited hospice patients, I only made one visit as many of them passed away before I could make a second visit a couple of weeks later. Many of them were comatose and were not necessarily conscious, so I didn't feel I could accurately assess what their emotional state was. I honestly felt like the dogs and I were making visits more for the families of the patients—families who were keeping vigil over their loved ones and relished being able to break away from their sadness to pet a dog and run their fingers through their long fur. I know it helped release tension in many family members.

Going back to the issue of required paperwork and making an assessment of the patient's emotional state, I had visited one hospice patient with Collin. The patient's daughter was there also, and she and I had a conversation while we tried to get the patient to pet Collin. To me, the patient seemed to be in a disagreeable mood, but when we left, her daughter caught me in the hall and said that that was the most positive she had seen her mother in months. I would have completed the paperwork all wrong by saying the patient was in a bad mood because to me she appeared that way when, in actuality, according to her daughter, she had a very positive experience.

I talked to the volunteer coordinator, and she said that the insurance company and, ultimately, Medicare required the paperwork be filled out. We discussed how therapy teams shouldn't be required to fill out that kind of paperwork as we were not hospice caregivers who get to know their patients on a very personal level and we are not professionals—nurses or doctors. She agreed but said there was nothing they could do about it as the government required it. I quit doing hospice work also because they started requiring hospice caregivers and, therefore, therapy dog teams to get an annual flu shot. I had had a pretty severe negative reaction to a flu shot in the late '80s, and I have vowed never to get another one. So for those reasons I stopped making hospice therapy visits.

Before Collin came into my life, I had started doing research about the quality of food available for dogs. I was horrified to find out the quality—or lack of quality—in the dog food I was feeding my dogs. I think of my dogs as my four-legged kids, and I want them to live long, healthy lives. In 2010 I had attended the Minnesota Wisconsin Collie Rescue annual dinner. Katie K-9 spoke at the dinner. She is a local radio personality hosting a show about canine and feline training and health. She had just published a cookbook for dogs, and that really got me to thinking. I had never considered cooking for my dogs or even feeding my dogs table scraps since the current thinking was that it was unhealthy for dogs to be given people food. But I think back to Tammy, my first sheltie, who lived to be sixteen and was fed nothing but table scraps, so maybe there was something to this. I purchased Katie's book and have been cooking what I call "toppers" for my dogs ever since. When I make toppers for my dogs, I always cook up a meat (chicken, liver, venison, ground beef); add vegetables; a grain such as quinoa or basmati rice; some fruit, such as blueberries or strawberries; and some other herbs and supplements. I have never gotten away from feeding kibbles, but I only feed high-quality dog kibble from a very few companies that I trust and then supplement that with a scoop of the topper, or every other night, the dogs get raw food as a topper from Raw Bistro, Steve's Raw Food, and Primal, to name a few.

Katie also talked about how we are overvaccinating our pets and suggested we pull titers on our animals. I had no idea what pulling titers was, so I decided to attend a Cooking for your Dog class that Katie K-9 and Dr. Jessica Levy, a holistic vet, offered. I learned a lot about how we do overvaccinate our pets. I've been having titers pulled for five years now, and every one of my dogs has displayed plenty of antibodies to fight against parvovirus, distemper, etc.

It was pretty apparent that Collin had been overvaccinated at the shelter in Wisconsin. His autoimmune disorder was a result of vaccinosis, or overvaccination. I understand that, when shelters get stray dogs in, they know nothing about these animals or if they are infected with contagious diseases or not. The routine is to give them several courses of shots in the course of a day or two. The problem is that vaccinations should never be given to a sick animal—their immune system cannot handle it. Also, dogs taken into a shelter are more than likely scared to death and extremely emotionally taxed, so their immune systems are not up to peak. In Collin's case, he was given multiple injections over a period of two days. That amount of vaccine obviously put his immune system in a tailspin and caused him to develop an autoimmune disorder. My hope is that all shelters, rescues, and veterinary offices will encourage pets to have titers pulled using a reasonably priced lab test that they can do in their own office and thereby save other pets from being needlessly overvaccinated.

In 2013, Collin's health started to decline. Besides the autoimmune disorder, he started having seizures and issues with his thyroid numbers. We put him on medication for the thyroid, but the seizures started happening more often and lasted longer each time. It broke my heart whenever he had a seizure because he couldn't control his body and sometimes thrashed about trying to stand up. I walked him home one afternoon from the groomer, whose shop was only a block away at that time. We were crossing a major highway when he started having a seizure. He couldn't control his legs, and I ended up having to literally drag him out of the intersection to safety.

The last six months of his life, Collin was extremely restless at night and was unable to control his bladder function. He had a severe seizure one night, and I rushed over to him to put my arms around him from the back to control the thrashing so he wouldn't get hurt, and he bit me. He had never done that before, and after the seizure was over, I could tell that, besides feeling exhausted, he felt bad about biting me.

I was having a terrible time trying to make the decision whether I should put him down or I should let him keep fighting. Collin had had another bad seizure early one Saturday morning in March of 2014. I sat at my computer that morning, and I looked over at Collin, who was staring out one of the sidelights of the front door. He had never done that before, and he just seemed out of sorts. I said to him, "Collin, if you feel it's your time, please let me know." Immediately after I said that, he walked over to me and sat down and just stared at me. He was telling me it was time.

I called the vet clinic, and they said to go right over. So we made our last drive together down Main Street to the vet clinic, where the vet very kindly and with much compassion sent Collin to the Rainbow Bridge. I cried for thirty minutes with him in my arms at the clinic. This noble dog who came to me with all sorts of scars on his nose and an autoimmune disease brought so much joy and smiles to everyone he met with his quiet, gentle nature. I know I will see Collin again someday, and I'm praying that he's running free with some of his other pals and Mario at the Rainbow Bridge.

CHAPTER TWELVE

Domino

In 2011, I had joined the Minnesota Sheltie Rescue. Since a sheltie was my first dog and I had had shelties my whole life, I felt I should try to help shelties in need. In June I received a call from the MN Sheltie Rescue, asking if I was willing to foster a little bi-black sheltie coming up from Iowa. I was told that he was very skittish and had been found wandering the streets of Des Moines when he was finally captured and taken into rescue. The family that had been fostering him in Iowa had to move, and they weren't able to take him with. I agreed to foster Domino.

Domino got along well with my pack, but he was very shy and scared of everything. When I would try to walk him, he acted as if he were totally overwhelmed, and he would shut down. The first week that Domino moved in, he had come up to me and wanted some food. I had been sitting on the couch, and the sunlight coming in through the window behind me showed what looked to be a cataract or some kind of covering over his right eye. I asked the rescue if I could take him to my vet, and they agreed.

My vet looked at his eye and agreed that there was definitely a cataract covering his right eye. She suggested I take Domino to a canine ophthalmologist in the Twin Cities to make sure everything was okay and if anything could be done about removing the cataract. I contacted the MN Sheltie Rescue, and they agreed to pay for Domino to go see Dr. Olivera.

Dr. Olivera spent a lot of time examining Domi's eyes. His diagnosis was that, first of all, Domi's right eye was smaller than the left—by quite a bit. And yes, when you do look at him, you can tell his right eye is smaller than the other. In Dr. Olivera's experience, he had done surgery to remove cataracts out of the smaller eyes in dogs but found that many of them were in quite a bit of pain afterward. He noted that Domi's cataract covered about three-fourths of his right eye and that during the day he would have vision only around the perimeter of the cataract as the pupil would be smaller because of the light of day. But in the evening, he would have much better vision as the pupil would be fully enlarged to let in more light. He did some more tests and found that the eye was healthy behind the cataract. His recommendation was to not do anything surgically on Domi and just let him live with his right eye as it was. So that was what was decided.

Domino was truly a frightened little boy, and knowing that he had limited vision on one side during the day, I surmised, helped in exasperating his fear. When I would take several of the dogs for a walk at the same time, Domino would constantly be looking over his right shoulder, expecting something to hurt him. One time when I was walking Mario and Harley on my left and Domino and Collin on my right, Collin came up on Domino's right side. Obviously, Domi hadn't seen him coming, but when he caught wind of something approaching him, he lashed out by attacking Collin. I realized then and there that Domino just wasn't a dog that would enjoy walks on the leash or being out in the big, wide world.

Domino had been with my "pack" for only three weeks when we had a severe thunderstorm blow through one Saturday morning. There were extremely strong winds behind this storm, so I waited until the storm had passed before letting the dogs out. I let them out into the backyard and then tried to fire up my computer, which I had shut down, fearing a power surge would destroy my computer. I was having an extremely difficult time getting my computer to start when it dawned on me that I hadn't heard the dogs barking at all. That was strange because they would often chase one another around the backyard, barking and herding their pack mates around the yard.

I went to the back door to see what the dogs were up to and, to my horror, found none of the dogs in the backyard. I could see that the back gate was slightly ajar—the wind must have blown it open. I hadn't checked to see if it was secure the night before. What a big mistake.

I rushed out to the backyard in a panic and started calling for all the dogs to come. Harley was a block over at the local farmers market, trying to weasel some food out of the vendors. He came back when I called him, so I shoved him into the house and went in search of the others.

Mario and Collin were across the street at a neighbor's. The neighbor was grilling hot dogs in his garage with the garage door halfway up. I should have known that my two dogs that never miss a meal would be over visiting someone grilling. I had grabbed the leashes, so I hooked up both Mario and Collin and escorted them home. Now I had to find Shelby and Domino.

Kids across the street from me said they had seen Shelby and Domino cross the street and head down the street adjacent to my house. I started running down that street, calling for both Shelby and Domi. Shelby had actually let the kids corral her until I could get there. I looked around though, but no Domino. I thanked the kids, hooked Shelby up, and marched her home.

Day 1

I realized that trying to track Domino was like looking for a needle in a haystack. I came back home and started making calls. First, I called the local police department and alerted them that Domino was on the run. Second, I called and left a message at the local animal shelter in case anyone was able to catch Domino and take him to the shelter. Third, I called the Minnesota Sheltie Rescue since Domino is technically their dog. I couldn't stop sobbing about Domino's escape. I know how shy and scared of people he is, and I know there were millions of places that Domino could find to hide in. Estelle and Karen from the sheltie rescue agreed to drive out just as soon as they could get there and help me pass out flyers, put up signs, and basically canvass the area where he was last seen.

Karen and Estelle arrived and spent the whole afternoon passing out flyers in the neighborhood and talking to people who might have seen Domino. I raced up and down Hassan Street, calling Domino's name. One neighbor told me she had seen Domino earlier by Faith Lutheran Church. After that, the trail went cold. No one I talked to had seen him. Karen had took out two live traps and showed me how to use them. I really hoped it wouldn't come to that. Karen and Estelle made the trek back to the Cities, and I sat down and couldn't stop crying. I felt so guilty about him getting away. Here the sheltie rescue had entrusted me with his care, and I let this sweet little guy slip through my fingers.

I decided to make my last call for the day. That call went to Ilga Cimbulis, an animal communicator. I had taken several classes with Ilga, and I found her to be very honest and forthright with her communications. She was more than willing to help me and told me she would connect with Domino and call me back. Fifteen minutes later, she called and said that Domino had passed by the following things: a church, a beauty salon, a gas station, and a body of water. Ilga indicated that he had headed southeast from my house. I told her I could verify the church, the gas station, and the body of water, but I couldn't remember there being a beauty salon anywhere southeast of my house. I thanked her for the information and told her I would call her later the next morning.

I couldn't sleep that night at all. I was so worried about Domino being out there alone. I knew he had survived alone on the streets in Des Moines, so he had some savvy on finding food and water. Still I worried about him being on the river. Coyotes and bobcats often follow rivers, and Domino wouldn't be able to survive a contest with a wild predator.

I had my cell phone placed right next to my pillow. About 1:00 a.m., I received a text saying they had seen Domino that evening and to text back. I responded with "Where did you see him and at what time?" The reply was that he was running down the road and he had a red paw and was limping. I asked which road they had seen him on. The reply was "Hassan Street." Hassan is the street where Shelby and Domino had run to from my house. I then asked what time the sighting was. The reply was "Nine fifteen that evening." Something seemed strange to me about the text. I had been out doing some searching for Domino myself after nine o'clock that evening, and it was starting to get dark enough that I know I wouldn't have been able to see if a dog running down the street had a red paw or not. I'm sure I would have noticed a dog limping, but the red paw seemed strange to me. I wanted to follow up on every lead, but I wasn't comfortable walking around the streets of town at one o'clock in the morning by myself. I emailed Estelle from the sheltie rescue about the text. She said that in the past, when a reward has been offered, some not-so-savory characters had appeared. She said I should go with my gut instincts and, if it didn't feel right, don't follow the lead—especially alone. I figured that four hours had passed already, and Domino was probably long gone from there if he had even been there at all.

Day 2

It was 4:30 a.m. and still dark out, but I decided to drive around in the car and follow the path that Ilga had seen Domino take. I drove past Faith Lutheran Church, where we had had two sightings the day before. Then I traveled east along Fourth Avenue to Adams Street, took a right, and went past the Cenex station on Adams. I continued a couple of blocks more along Adams Street and came to the bridge crossing the Crow River. The city had been doing construction on Adams Street from the bridge south to Airport Road. So there was no "through" traffic on the road. The area is all industrial on this part of Adams Street. The huge 3M plant is on the east side of Adams, and on the west side are several businesses—construction companies, excavating companies, the armory building, and the city's park maintenance building. I got out and tried calling Domino to me. Nothing!

I came to the conclusion that my driving around looking for Domino was probably not the best use of my time. I decided to take a different way back to my house, and lo and behold, there was a beauty salon just one block away from me. I had forgotten all about it. I couldn't wait to talk to Ilga to give her validation of everything she said Domino had seen the day before.

My friend Terry went out to help me look for Domino. We went for breakfast, and then I called Ilga to tell her I could verify the beauty salon. Ilga had me drive over to a road that I had never heard of before—Ranch Ave. It was just east/south of the Crow River. Ilga told me that Domino had drunk from a marsh area on this road and that there would be a cluster of five or six 1960s–1970s homes. We drove over to Ranch Avenue, and sure enough, there was a marsh next to the road, and to the east were five homes all of 1960s to 1970s vintage. I left a flyer at each home, but no one had seen Domino. Ilga told me to concentrate my efforts in this area. On the other side of the river from Ranch Avenue is the 3M plant. We pulled into 3M, and I went in to talk to the guards at the guardhouse. They took a flyer, and one of them told me he had seen Domino the day before, running down Oakland Avenue straight toward the 3M plant. Good news, we had another sighting and more validation for Ilga's communications. We went back to my house as some more volunteers from the sheltie rescue were coming over with additional signs to be placed around town.

My friend Terry had to leave for home, so I decided to pass out flyers to all the homes around the 3M plant. As I did, several of the people I talked to said they had just received an automated call talking about Domino and the phone numbers to call if anyone should sight him. Wow, the sheltie rescue is really organized. I finished passing out flyers and went home to take care of my dogs.

Debbie, a member of the spaniel rescue, drove out five more signs that she had made up. What a sweet person to drive all the way out from the cities to deliver the signs. I knew exactly where I was going to place the signs tomorrow.

Day 3

I had to go to work on Monday. Thankfully, Monday and Wednesday are only half days in the morning. I had talked to Ilga on Monday morning, and she said that Domino had come across some kind of a concrete barrier and had gone under a wire fence and had scraped his face a bit while doing so. Once I got home from work, I decided to go over to 3M and get permission to walk their property along both banks of the river and to place a live trap. I stopped again at the guardhouse and talked to the two guards inside. One of them said he had also seen Domino on Saturday, running like the devil was after him toward the 3M plant. We had a second sighting of Domino in the same area.

I got the number of the manager at 3M who could give me permission to walk the property. He was in a meeting, so I had to leave a message. I decided to just walk the property anyway. I walked along the north shore of the river between the cyclone fence encircling the 3M property and the Crow River. I forged my own path in trying to find any sign of Domino having been through the area. I got about half a mile in when I came to a large concrete pier that went down to the river. I walked up to the river's edge and saw both raccoon tracks and dog tracks. I felt positive that Domino had been here sometime in the last two days.

Another volunteer from the sheltie rescue, Judith, drove down to help me look for Domino. She also had brought additional signs to place in strategic spots in town. I decided to place a live trap in the area, but I wasn't comfortable with placing it on 3M property until I heard back from my contact at 3M. I figured I would place the trap across Adams Street from 3M but still along the river. I got permission from the company owning the land, and Judith and I set up the trap, baiting it with one of my stinky T-shirts, some Grandma Lucy's chicken dinner, and Domino's Kong toy filled with peanut butter. I had called my ex-husband, who lives less than a mile from me. When we were first married, he trapped as an avocation and made good money at it. Unfortunately, styles change, and fur went out of favor. But I knew he was knowledgeable about releasing animals from traps. He agreed to help me release any critter that I caught in the live trap that wasn't Domino! Everything was set!

I had planned on checking the traps at midnight and at 4:00 a.m. To be honest, I was feeling exhausted by now. I had been living on adrenaline and about two hours of sleep the past two nights. I was communicating with the sheltie rescue via Facebook and email. Estelle emailed, saying that a local policeman had sighted a large black-and-white sheltie in a trailer park in the northwest section of town. It was my responsibility to follow up on any sightings although my heart wasn't in it. I believed in my heart that Domino was somewhere southeast of my home down along the river. Ilga had seen Domino confront certain buildings and landmarks that he would have if he had gone in a southeast direction from my house. But I felt the obligation to check it out, so at midnight I took Harley, one of my collies, with me to check the trap and to walk the trailer court. There was nothing in the trap, and walking the trailer court at one o'clock in the morning didn't produce a single dog sighting, much less a sheltie sighting.

After checking the trap at midnight, I decided to just stay awake and watch TV so I would be sure to not fall asleep and miss out on checking the trap again at 4:00 a.m. As I lay in bed, watching *I Love Lucy*, I saw something flutter in front of the TV screen. My first thought was that I had a large moth in the house. I turned on the light and realized that I had a bat in the bedroom. The bat was frenetic with its flying movements, diving close to me but not touching me. I panicked and scooted all the dogs out of the bedroom. I had heard you can use a tennis racket to hit a bat. Unfortunately, I didn't have a tennis racket, but what I did have was the baby gate at the top of the steps. It had a diamond pattern in it like a tennis racket. I shooed the bat into the bathroom (or so I thought) and shut the door. Then I ran downstairs and looked up on the internet how to remove a bat from a house. It said to confine it to one room, open all the windows in that room, and try to move it toward the open window. I don't have windows that open like that. Great.

I gathered up my heavy gardening gloves, a pullover top with a hood and some jeans, grabbed the baby gate, and slowly opened the bathroom door. Nothing. I pounded on all the hanging pictures and items in the bathroom, but I wasn't able to get the bat to fly out. I walked back into the bedroom and didn't see the bat. I was so tired at this time that I figured I must have had a waking nightmare and hallucinated about the bat.

In any case, I lay back down in bed to watch TV again—after all, I still had two hours to go before I wanted to check the live trap. I still had *I Love Lucy* on and had just settled down to watch when the bat reappeared. I turned on the light, opened up the door to the balcony off my bedroom and left it open, grabbed the baby gate, and tried moving the bat to the open door. Finally, the bat flew out the door. One crisis averted!

Day 4

Finally, it was 4:00 a.m., time to go check the trap. I drove out to the trap and approached it in the dark. I had caught something, and it was black and white. Unfortunately, it wasn't Domino, but a skunk. Good grief, how was I going to get a skunk out of the trap? I thought about calling my ex, but even I'm not mean enough to call up my ex at four o'clock in the morning and ask him to release a skunk. And to be honest, I felt that, since Domino had gotten lost on my watch, I needed to do whatever it took to get him back. Nope, it was up to me to figure out how to get that skunk out of the trap.

I raced back home and did an internet search on releasing a skunk from a live trap. Apparently, the trick is to bring several towels to cover the trap in the event the skunk should spray, to open the trap door, and to place a piece of wood to keep the door open and then leave. The skunk will leave on its own once it feels safe. I gathered up three towels, my heavy gardening gloves (used with the bat last night), and headed out to release the skunk. By the time I got there, it was daylight, and it was impossible to approach the trap without the skunk seeing me. He sprayed before I got close enough to throw the towels over the trap. Yuck, what a stink. I still threw the towels over the trap, raised the door, put the piece of wood in place to keep the door open and went home to take a shower and wash my hair. I'd bait the trap again after work that afternoon. I hoped I didn't clear the room at my two Tuesday workplaces because of the skunk smell!

I continued posting updates on Domino's disappearance on my Facebook page. Many of my local friends were doing their best to keep an eye out for any sign of Domino. Several of my friends were even biking close to the river in an effort to track him. Updating Domino's status was one of the things I used to keep my sanity. I was so thrilled with the number of Facebook friends who were trying their best to help me find Domino!

I went to both of my Tuesday bookkeeping jobs. It was hard for me to concentrate because all I could think of was Domino and how frightened he must be. I left my afternoon job about three o'clock and decided to again walk along the river on 3M's property since I had finally received permission to walk the property on both sides of the river and to set a live trap. I walked down Ranch Avenue almost all the way to the Adams Street bridge. I took pictures of the area with my cell phone so I could send them to Ilga via Facebook. I hoped she would get a better feel of where Domino had been.

I checked the trap, and thank heaven, the skunk had left the trap. I had to throw away the towels and my T-shirt because of the skunk stink. I also had to leave my shoes and gloves outside to try to bake the stench out of them in the sun. I put another towel in the trap and some stinky food inside in hopes of drawing Domino into the trap.

I had decided I needed some sleep, so I opted to check the trap at ten o'clock and again at 6:00 a.m. Hopefully, there wouldn't be any more bat sightings, and I could get a few hours of sleep. I watched some TV, took a bath, threw my clothes on, checked the trap, and found nothing. At least I could go home and get some sleep.

Day 5

At last I got about five hours of sleep last night. I woke up and checked the trap first thing. There was good news and bad news. The good news is that I didn't catch another skunk. The bad news is that I hadn't caught Domino. Hope dies hard though, and I really felt that I was close to where he was hiding.

I got off work at eleven o'clock. I decided to place the second live trap somewhere along the Ranch Avenue area. While I was struggling to get the trap in my car, I received a phone call from PJ and Tim, Domino's Iowa foster family. They were on their way up from

Iowa to lend their hand in helping to find Domino. Wow, I was so impressed with all the help I had received. Tim agreed to help me get the second live trap set up.

Once PJ and Tim arrived, we walked the area where Ilga felt Domino was roaming. We called for him, begging him to show himself. PJ called for Cody to come out in hopes that he would remember his name while he was in her care and remember her voice. We spent several hours walking the area, calling for Cody/Domino, but we didn't have a single sighting. It was so disappointing. At least the second trap was set, and hopefully, Domino would be hungry enough to walk into the trap if he was within range of the smell of the bait.

After Tim and PJ left (and bless their hearts for the heroic effort to help find Domino), I decided to run to the local Menards to buy a couple of sign frames for the two signs I had sitting at my house that didn't have frames. While in Menards, I ran into the couple who built my fence. I told them my dogs had escaped my backyard. I had had the fence gates made to automatically close and latch, but the previous winter was so harsh that the gates would not automatically close anymore. They agreed to come over and reset the post or do whatever it took to get the gates to close—one less worry for me.

Debbie, from the spaniel rescue, who had brought signs out on Sunday, called to say she was coming out this evening to pass out flyers. She needed to know what areas had already received flyers and what areas needed to be canvassed. I gave her a map and told her that I hadn't done anything in the southwest part of the city. So she set out with flyers in hand to distribute them in the southwest part of town. I grabbed a bunch of flyers and headed out to the trailer park in the northwest part of town, where the policeman had called with a sighting of a large black-and-white sheltie.

The evening was hot and humid, and it took every bit of energy I had to walk up and down the streets of the trailer park. But I did it, and I stopped and talked to as many people as I could. Those people I did talk to had not seen any loose dogs in the area for weeks, but they agreed to call me if they should see one.

By the time I got back home, Debbie had finished up passing out quite a few flyers and was ready to head home. We talked about lost dogs (she had previously lost a spaniel that she dearly loved) and the use of animal communicators in helping to find lost pets. She also gave me some tips to help others in the continuing search for Domino.

I went out at ten o'clock to check both traps, and there was nothing in them—again, a good news/bad news situation. I came back home, took a hot bath, and went to bed and slept until 6:00 a.m.

Day 6

I called Ilga in the morning, and she said that she kept getting that Domino was still alive and that he kept rambling back and forth over the river area by the 3M plant. I felt good that we had the traps in good places to try to lure him in.

I went to work and came home for lunch. I had used my cell phone quite a bit in the morning, so I plugged it in to recharge. I grabbed lunch and ran out the door to my afternoon job. When I got to the workplace, I realized I had left my cell phone at home plugged into the charger. I hurried through my job tasks and raced home to check my phone. Sure enough—there was a voicemail message from a local number that I didn't recognize.

The message was from a City of Hutchinson employee who worked at the park maintenance building on Adams Street, just south of the river. He said he had seen Domino dart out of the marsh area fronting the river. He called to him, but Domino ran back into the marsh. He then called me. I can't believe I didn't have my phone with me, because the call came in about ten minutes after I had left home. By now it was a couple of hours later. I was so thrilled though to have had another Domino sighting and that he was truly still alive. I grabbed Harley, and we drove down to the park maintenance building.

Adams Street from the bridge passing over the Crow River south to Airport Road was under construction. The center two lanes were completed and were made of concrete, which sat about eight inches higher than the current shoulders, which were down to the dirt at this point. To get to the park building, I carefully drove my car down from the concrete level onto the dirt shoulder and into the parking lot of the park building. Harley and I walked all around the marsh area all the time, calling for Domino. Nothing again! Harley is normally a very talkative collie, but I couldn't get him to make a peep.

Even though we weren't able to get Domino to come out, I still felt good because we had had a sighting. I decided to go get the second live trap that was over off Ranch Avenue and set it up right by the marsh area. I slowly "climbed" back onto the eight-inch concrete center lanes of Adams Street, dropped Harley back home, and drove over to Ranch Avenue to get the second trap.

I grabbed the trap and hauled it back to my car; however, for some reason my car looked lopsided. Oh well. I threw the trap in the back and started the engine. Once the engine was running, the tire pressure trouble light came on. I got out and looked around the car, and sure enough, the right front passenger tire was flat. It must have happened when going down or climbing back up on the concrete lanes of the construction on Adams Street.

Changing a flat tire has never been part of my job description. I called Gary at one of my bookkeeping jobs and asked him if he might be able to come and help me change my flat tire. He came over to help me and had the tire changed in less than five minutes. Thank the Lord I have a full-size spare tire. I thanked Gary and drove over to my afternoon bookkeeping job, a tire shop. They tested the tire, and unfortunately, it wasn't a puncture that could be repaired. It was a bruise, and the tire was beyond repair, and I would have to buy a new tire that would have to be ordered and sent out. They tightened the lug nuts on the spare tire, and I was on my way again.

This time, I drove up to the construction on Adams Street and just carried the live trap over to the area where I wanted to set it. I put some more stinky food in it along with a towel and another one of Domino's toys. Everything was ready. Now all Domino had to do was walk into one of the traps.

I felt pretty positive that Domino was going to walk into one of the traps in the next day or two. I still had quite a few flyers left that Debbie had brought out last night, so I decided to canvass every house on the other side of the river from Domino's last sighting, Jefferson Street. Although Debbie had told me to just deliver the flyers, I wanted to knock on people's doors and ask them to look out for Domino since he had been sighted just across the river from their house. I figured he might try to come up and get into a garbage can or two since I knew he had to be starving by now.

Everything was going well when I was passing out flyers. Many people mentioned that they had seen the signs up about Domino in town and said they would call if they should see him. I was approaching one house that was set back quite a bit from the road. It was just about opposite the riverbank from where Domino was seen, so I definitely wanted to talk to the owners. I got about halfway down the driveway when four dogs came running out at me—two springer/pointer type dogs, one dog that looked like Benji, and a rottweiler. All four were barking, but I was so determined to talk to the people that I just kept forging on. The rottweiler came up behind me and bit me hard on the butt. I couldn't believe it—the stupid dog actually bit me when all I was doing was walking. Needless to say, I turned around and walked back out. The next-door neighbor's daughter saw it happen and offered me a ride home. I told her "Thanks," but I wanted to finish up handing out flyers. My butt actually felt better the more that I walked.

When I got home, I checked the bite in a mirror. I already had a huge (four-inch) black bruise, and the bite had broken the skin in three places. Obviously, the dogs were confined by invisible fence, which I hate. Sorry if I am offending any invisible fence users, but that type of fencing only keeps your dog confined, and that's only if the fence is working. They do have a habit of not functioning. Plus, some dogs are willing to take the jolt of electricity to get to the other side if they're chasing something like a rabbit or squirrel. Invisible fence does nothing to keep out other animals and people. These homeowners are basically a lawsuit waiting to happen. I can only imagine what would happen if a child in the development next door went running on their property to chase a ball.

The dog bite put a damper on the rest of my evening, but I tried to remain hopeful that Domino would be caught soon. I tried to do some animal communication of my own with Domino to *not* go onto that property. Domino would have made a tasty morsel for the rottweiler if he should be found sneaking on the property. I prayed Domino would not venture to the other side of the river!

Day 7

I got up at midnight and at 5:00 a.m. to check the traps. I caught nothing! Again, it was a good news/bad news situation. No skunk caught, but no Domino either. I just knew he had to be close by, but I didn't know how to draw him out.

I came back home after checking the traps early this morning and decided to lounge around in bed, listening to a morning radio show. I didn't have to be anywhere until ten o'clock when the singing group I'm in had a scheduled practice for an upcoming gig. I was nodding off a little while listening to the radio when my phone rang about 7:30 a.m. The caller was another employee of the City of Hutchinson park department, and he had just seen Domino pop out of the marsh behind the park maintenance building but on the other side of the fence, closer to the armory. I thanked him for the call, grabbed Harley again, and made the five-minute drive to the building in three minutes.

Harley and I walked all around the marsh again while I called for Domino to come out. We walked almost a mile south on the dirt road that parallels the river, all the while calling for him. I still couldn't get him to come out. I decided to head back home and reset the traps. I called Estelle at the sheltie rescue to tell her that we had had another Domino sighting, but I still couldn't get him to come out of hiding. Estelle told me that I would probably have better luck getting Domino with the traps. Just as she said that, I happened to glance back at the marsh area. Right at that moment, Domino popped out of the marsh like a bat out of hell. I told Estelle I saw him and I would call her back. Harley and I ran back down to the marsh area.

By the time Harley and I got back down there, Domino had gone back into the tall reeds of the marsh. I called for him to come out for five minutes, but he wouldn't come out. I know he heard me, so he must have been too frightened to feel comfortable coming out of the shadows of the tall grass. I decided to sit down in the grass and just wait and see if Domino would resurface. Harley was still on leash, but he wandered around me in a circle. Just as I was about to give up on Domino being able to overcome his fear of people, he darted back out into the open about fifteen feet away from me. I was so excited to see him I called to him in a quiet voice. He stopped, looked at me, looked totally startled, and then saw Harley and bounded over to Harley with his tail wagging. I still couldn't get him to come near me, but I just let him have fun with Harley.

I continued to call him to me, and he would come close, but not close enough for me to grab him. I finally decided to lie down in the grass. I called Harley over to me, and Domino followed him. I continued to talk to Domino in a quiet voice, telling him how much I had missed him and how glad I was to see him. After a couple of minutes of me lying prone on the grass and Harley and Domino moving around me, Domino finally came up by my face, sat down, and let out a huge sigh. I scooped him up in my arms, and thus ended Domino's big adventure!

The minute I got home with Domino, I called Estelle and told her the wonderful news. We both were crying and feeling joyous over Domino's return home. I brought Domino into the house, and he was happily reunited with Shelby, Collin, and Mario. I think all of them were happy to see him—well, all of them except Mario. Estelle told me to take Domino into the vet for a check and to ask them to run blood tests and check for signs in case he had gotten into any rat poison—something another lost sheltie had gotten into while roaming in an industrial part of town.

The vet's office told me to bring him right over and they would "work on him" while I was at rehearsal. I have never sung with more joy than I did this Friday morning after finding Domino. My heart was so overjoyed and grateful that I had this little dog back home! I picked up Domino after rehearsal and got the news that he seemed none the worse for wear from his adventure other than losing about three pounds—three pounds on Domino is a lot, but I knew I could get him back in shape in no time.

I called Estelle once I was back home from the vet's office with Domino and gave her the news. I also told her that I had decided to adopt Domino—I didn't want this wonderful little dog to build up trust with me and then have to go to another family and start over as far as trust goes. I had missed Domino so much that I really wanted him to be a permanent fixture in my life. Things have been slow going with Domino, and I'm hoping he'll learn to trust me and feel comfortable and secure. But Domino has made great strides in overcoming his fears. And one thing for sure about Domino is that he is truly loved by me and the rest of the pack!

CHAPTER THIRTEEN

Skylar

I had retired Collin in 2013 because of his worsening health conditions. I do like to have multiple therapy dogs to choose from when making a visit. For doing demonstrations and dances, you can't beat Harley. When visiting the elderly, a quieter dog is needed. Late summer of 2013, I was again perusing the Puppyfind website, looking at available sheltie pups. Staring out from one of the ads was a picture of a precious black-and-white sheltie lying on a beach lounge. She obviously had blue merle somewhere in her background, but this little girl was only black and white—mostly white. She had a split face with one side of her face being black with a bright blue eye, and the other side was white with a beautiful brown eye. As I read further into the description of this puppy, the breeder said the puppy was deaf. I had never trained or had a deaf dog before. Hmm, was I up for the challenge?

I contacted the breeder, who said she was horrified when the litter of puppies was born in July of 2013—three were bi-black boys and then this little white girl. She had had her tested for hearing, and the results were that she was bilaterally deaf. This means that Skylar doesn't have hearing in either ear. The breeder also said that this puppy had such a sweet, loving personality, and she was hoping that whoever purchased her would be willing to use her for therapy work. Those were the magic words, so I purchased Skylar sight unseen and had her flown up to Minnesota in early November 2013.

Handling live cargo protocol had changed since I had Harley flown up from Kentucky in 2008. Instead of going to one of the cargo buildings, Skylar was placed in a cargo area inside the main terminal at the Minneapolis airport. I was so excited for her to come that I got there early and had to wait for twenty minutes while they took all the live cargo off the plane. At last I could see Skylar—an incredibly precious puppy with a look of confusion on her face. She came in a pretty good-sized crate, and I was having difficulty carrying it without jarring her too much. A wonderful African American skycap came over and volunteered to take Skylar out to the car and lift the crate into my car off his flatbed cart. He was so helpful to me and fascinated by the fact that Skylar is deaf. I gave him a very nice tip and headed home with my new little girl.

Skylar spent her first few months in the house adjusting to her fellow siblings and to get acquainted with the layout of the house and how we did things, such as when feeding time was, using the backyard for going potty, and potty training in general. Skylar is very bright, and she caught on quickly to how things ran in the household.

I was anxious to get her started on basic obedience training, but I first took her to one of our therapy dog group meetings. She was so cute and snuggly that not a whole lot got accomplished at the meeting because everyone was passing Skylar around and just cuddling her. She seemed to relish being held and petted by people and even being passed around—the mark of a future therapy dog. I was very pleased after this meeting.

We didn't start actual obedience training until April of 2014. Before training, I had accessed several deaf-dog websites on how to train dogs and purchased several books on training deaf dogs. Since the dog can't hear you give commands, hand signals would be the key to training obedience commands. I read these books several times faithfully and determined what hand signals I would use to indicate heel, sit, down, stay, and come. These are the basic commands that the dog must perform in order to pass the therapy dog test, and so those are the ones I concentrated on.

The first week was a debacle for me. In obedience, you are always working with the dog on your left side. I found it difficult to give Skylar the hand signal with my left hand, hold the leash with the other hand, and find a hand to reach in my pocket and get a treat out for reward when she did things correctly. Plus, I'm not a kid anymore, and reaching down to sheltie height to give the heel command was not necessarily the most acrobatic maneuver I could do. The actual signal for heel that I use is given by holding my left arm straight down with my fingers extended and then bending the arm at the elbow and swinging it up. Sometimes Skylar would get the cue, and sometimes not. At the beginning also, there were several times I probably pulled on the collar more than I should have (or more than I wanted to) in order to get her attention.

Collars—what type of collar should I use on a sweet little deaf sheltie girl? I looked at the many different types—buckle, prong, halti or gentle leader, choke chain—and decided on a martingale. Martingales work on the principle that they will tighten up just enough so that the dog cannot back out of it. I know of several dogs (my own included) who have slipped regular buckle collars, and in some cases, these dogs became runaways. Martingale collars are made of all nylon and some with chain for the part that tightens up on the neck. I knew I wanted a martingale because, if my deaf little girl ever slipped her collar, she might be totally frightened and run. She wouldn't be able to hear me calling for her, so I wanted a collar that I felt comfortable that she couldn't slip. I found the perfect martingale collar for her in purple (of course my favorite color), and off we went to training.

Skylar and I stumbled along for five of the six weeks of beginning obedience training. Some weeks she would do better, and some she acted like she didn't have a clue what I was asking of her. I was feeling frustrated and like a failure. Luckily, the local Pet Walk for our local shelter was held the weekend before our final week of class. Ilga Cimbulis, my animal communicator friend who had helped in getting Domino back home, had a booth at this event. So did the Minnesota Wisconsin Collie Rescue and our local TDI chapter.

I took Sky along with me to the event and sat down with Ilga for a reading. What I wanted Ilga to ask Skylar was what could I do to improve things in our training and if she wanted to be a therapy dog. What Ilga got from her were two pretty important points: I was too slow giving her the signals and way too slow giving her the treat reward. Also, Ilga got from Skylar that she has difficulty seeing out of one of her eyes. Well, this was interesting news to me, and I'm pretty sure the information Ilga got was 100 percent correct. When I had Skylar home later in the afternoon, I tested her eyes to see if she had any vision impairment. I found that her right eye (her blue eye) didn't blink until I had my finger almost up to it. Since she is on my left when we are doing obedience, this is the eye that would see (or, in her case, probably not see) any hand signals given.

The following week on the last night of class, I decided to really exaggerate my hand signals and be sure that I had a treat in my hand before we started any of the exercises. Skylar nailed every one of them. This is the second time Ilga has given me correct information. I have no doubt that Ilga has the ability to communicate with animals and get useful information from them.

So Skylar and I finished up the six-week obedience class on a high note. I decided to take the summer off from training and start again in the fall closer to the therapy dog classes. I used the beginner obedience class as a refresher for Skylar to get the basics down pat before we started in on working on making visits, dealing with hospital equipment, and walking in a crowd.

Sky remembered everything from the first Beginning Obedience I class from four months prior, so we whizzed right through that class. Next was the Therapy Dog training classes, and I was so looking forward to them but had a huge conflict. This time they were scheduled for Tuesday evenings, and I work every Tuesday evening with the Adaptive Recreation group. I run the Adaptive Rec program, and there was no time to find someone to fill in for me so I could attend the therapy dog training classes. So I decided to stay home and work with Skylar in the basement on the therapy dog issues—away from the rest of the pack.

We would practice every day for fifteen to twenty minutes in the basement, first heeling and then stopping and sitting. I hooked her up to a long line (a horse lunge line actually), had her sit, stay, and then walked to the end of the line, where I had her stay for a while—even up to a minute. Then I would walk back to her and reward her for a job well done, or instead of me walking back to her, I would signal her to come. Getting her to carry that heavy lunge line was a problem, but she had to get used to it to be able to pass the TDI test. For four weeks straight we practiced various commands such as "Sit stay," "Down stay," and "Come." I was able to attend one of the therapy dog classes, and so I was able to do a meet and greet, walk through a crowd with some of the crowd behaving strangely, and pretend to make an actual visit. By the time of the test though, I was still pretty nervous.

I can remember the first time I had tested with Tim as an evaluator. I was so nervous, and I should have remembered from raising horses that my nervousness goes straight down the leash to the dog just as horses can pick up through the saddle that you are fearful. Tim told me to relax a couple of times when testing Harley, and when I did pass with him, I was ecstatic. It got easier each time—with Mario and Collin, but I had never tested a deaf dog before, and I was a little uncomfortable with how the test would go as TDI had changed their test format.

The Saturday morning for the test dawned bright, and I was anxious to take Skylar to EZ Obedience for her test. We were the second team to test, and I decided to just relax, be exuberant with my signals for Skylar, and pray that she didn't get up during the sit stay or down stay until I gave her the signal. She came through the test perfectly. I was so proud of her that I honestly felt that Christmas had come early for me. I couldn't wait to get my paperwork in and get our badge and bandana for Sky so we could make visits.

TDI requires an annual vet visit for the dog along with a fecal exam. At that time I had five dogs in the house, and I honestly didn't know where each one of them did their business. So the morning of Skylar's exam, I grabbed a sheltie-size poop and headed to the vet's office. They pulled titers on Sky and found everything was good, her rabies vaccination was up-to-date, but the bad news was that she had worms in her poop. I was crushed. None of my dogs had ever tested positive for worms (remember I had three therapy dogs and they each had to have a fecal exam every year), and the saying goes that, if one dog has them, they all do. The vet gave me medication for Skylar to take and told me to have her tested again in three weeks after she had taken all the medication.

I figured out that it was probably one of Domino's poops that I had taken into the vet's office as he has a habit of eating poop. I'm sure that comes from being on the run for almost a year down in Iowa and trying to find food to eat before he was taken into rescue. Dogs will eat feces if they are starving, and Domino has never gotten out of the habit. But the fact is that it's a good thing I did grab one of Domi's poops because it alerted me to the fact that all the dogs could have worms. Every one of the dogs got the wormer medication, and after three weeks, I took Sky in to be tested. Everything was clear—yippee!

I turned in my paperwork, the medical papers, and my check to get Skylar registered. Within three weeks, I had my badge and bandanna in hand, and we were able to start making visits together. We started making visits at our local nursing home. Harmony River had just been built the year before and was a beautiful facility containing eight neighborhoods. Every visit, we would visit four of the neighborhoods as I found that an hour to an hour and a half was all the time that Skylar could handle making visits.

I inform the people that we visit that Skylar is deaf, and they are so amazed by her ability to respond to hand signals and become a therapy dog. People love to sink their fingers into her thick, soft fur, and she accommodates them by just standing there. Sometimes I will lift her so wheelchair-bound people can pet her. People are also fascinated by her one blue eye and her one brown eye. Her coloring is unique, and people are mesmerized by her.

I had a great time training Skylar, and I love her for her quiet demeanor when we make visits. In the fall of 2015, we visited at the Litchfield Library for children to "read" to the dogs. One little boy liked Skylar and enclosed her in a huge hug. I was a little nervous about it because I know Mario had not done well when exposed to a bear hug. But Skylar took it in stride and actually gave the boy a kiss. Skylar was turning out to be a wonderful therapy dog, but I began to think about how I can use her deafness to help other people. I contemplated on that question while I continued to make visits with Skylar throughout 2015.

CHAPTER FOURTEEN

Olaf

On a cold February day in 2015, Olaf made the journey from New York to Minnesota. The day picked for the transport was Saturday, February 7. Olaf's foster mom drove him to Pennsylvania the night before. Bright and early on February 7, Olaf made the trek from Pennsylvania to Eau Claire, Wisconsin, where I picked him up. All day long, each transporter posted pictures of Olaf on his journey to Minnesota. I was getting so excited to see this beautiful blue-eyed boy.

Two of my good friends, Kitty and Arnie, made the journey to Eau Claire with me, and it's a good thing they did. Olaf finally made it to Eau Claire around 7:45 p.m., where he bounded out of the transporter's car and over to me. As I said earlier, I figured he had to be hungry after being on the road for so long, so I offered him one of Kitty's homemade turkey jerky treats. He nearly tore my fingers off. Right at that moment, I knew that I was going to have my hands full training with this dog.

On the way back to Minnesota, Olaf sat in the back seat with Arnie. However, Olaf could smell the doggy bag of food that Kitty had brought from the restaurant where we had dinner before traveling on to Eau Claire. Olaf kept fidgeting and tried to get to the front seat so he could get some of that wonderful-smelling food. A couple of times I noticed that it was really cold in the car even though I had the heater running at full blast. It turns out Olaf was so wiggly that Arnie was having a difficult time keeping him from stepping on the electric window openers. Thank God, Kitty and Arnie were there to keep Olaf in check.

I have fostered quite a few collies for the MWCR, and I have a set routine for introducing new dogs to my pack. First I drive into my garage and lower the garage door. Then I let the new dog out of the car into the backyard to sniff and run around for ten or fifteen minutes. After they've gotten used to the backyard, I let out my pack. No one is on a leash as that can cause issues for the dog that's on leash. I have to admit that my pack is really well-balanced, and they have accepted every single foster dog I've brought into the house. But I was somewhat nervous about blending Olaf into the pack at night. I liked to be able to see what's happening with the interaction of my dogs. I didn't need to worry. He and Skylar formed an instant connection. I don't know if their bond comes from the fact that they are both deaf or if their energy flow is on the same level, but they formed an instant attraction to each other.

Olaf is a very independent dog. He has his own way of thinking. I had gotten used to Skylar's quiet and reserved nature, so I had assumed that Olaf would be the same. Olaf proved to me that assuming anything with him was a mistake. For starters, Olaf is a counter surfer. A week after his arrival, I had baked two lemon loaf cakes for an event that I was attending. I had left them on the oven to cool before I frosted them. Big mistake! I was out in the living room, watching TV with the other dogs gathered around me. I didn't see Olaf among the pack all stretched out on the floor around the sofa. I couldn't call for him because he wouldn't hear me, so I started to look for him. I found him in the kitchen, happily munching on lemon loaf cake. He honestly had the silliest grin on his face as he inhaled one of the cakes and one half of the other one. Needless to say, I wasn't a happy camper, and I learned right away that I would need to "Olaf-proof" the house.

So what do I mean by Olaf-proof? That meant that no food-stuffs could be left on the counters, tables, side tables, oven top, and even the rolling wood butcher block table was no obstacle for him. When it comes to food, Olaf knows no limits. I don't know if some of the absolute need to ingest all foodstuffs in the house comes from experiences in his past or if he just has that big of a hunger or need.

Olaf has also counter-surfed and pulled books from off my tables and desks. These too he looks at as edible fodder. I have lost a total of five books to Olaf's endless need to taste new and different items. He's even eaten some of my favorite books by mystery author Dorothy Bodoin. She writes lighthearted mysteries, all of which contain collies and collie rescue. For Olaf to have eaten three of Dorothy's books and still be alive to talk about it tells you how much I really do love this little guy.

Olaf is also a prankster. I like to take a hot bath every night, filling the tub with Epsom salts and lavender and sinking into the water with a good book. It's one of the few ways I allow myself to relax. However, Olaf looks at my bath time as a means for challenging me and getting attention. One time I had finished a chapter in the book I was reading and decided to put the book down in the basket next to the tub and just close my eyes and relax. Within a minute, I heard a rustling sound next to the tub and opened my eyes to see Olaf had grabbed the book I had been reading and was now proudly prancing out the bathroom door with it. This book was a library book, so I needed to get it from Olaf's clutches before he chewed it to shreds. Running through the house naked, covered with a towel, I finally tracked down Olaf before he had a chance to take a couple of bites out of it.

Another time, I was lounging in the tub, reading a good book, when Olaf came and stood by the tub, bent down and grabbed my towel, and took off running. Believe me, it wasn't a pretty picture of me chasing him through the house wet and dripping all over the hardwood floors. Yup, he's a prankster, all right.

At the time Olaf joined the household, I crated Domino and Skylar when I would leave for the day. Whenever a new dog comes into the household, whether it is a foster or permanent resident, I like to crate them when I feed them and also crate them when I go to work. Crating Olaf while feeding him is the best thing I could have done. He did and still does inhale his food, and then he runs around and tries to take food from the other dogs. He didn't dare try to take food from Harley, Shelby, or Mario—they have let him know in no uncertain terms that their food dish is off-limits to him. But Skylar and Domino are less-dominant dogs, and Olaf could easily push them off their dishes. While I hate having the crates in my living room (except for Domino's, which is actually a wooden piece of furniture), until Olaf can eat his dinner and not exploit his sheltie siblings, I will continue to feed him in the crate. Just some of the tricks you learn when you have dogs.

When Olaf came into my household, it was obvious that all my dogs each had different personalities. But Olaf really brought home to me how different they each are. Olaf is intelligent but extremely independent. He's affectionate and likes to lie close to me when I'm working at the computer or watching TV, but he does not like to give kisses the way Harley, Shelby, and Skylar do. He absolutely refuses to give kisses. Another difference in personality is the length of his attention span. Skylar could go all hour long in our obedience classes and still be able to pay attention. With Olaf, about thirty-five to forty minutes into class, he would start looking around, licking his chops, and had totally zoned out as far as paying attention to commands. Just a few of the differences I observed with Olaf.

Olaf and I attended Beginning Obedience at our local training facility. He did fairly well but had a very difficult time with sitting and staying. He could do the down-stay much better than Skylar could, but the sit-stay seemed to be more than he could deal with. We begin teaching the sit-stay by sitting the dog, giving them the signal to stay, which in this case meant putting my left hand in front of his face and eyes, and then stepping out on the right foot and pivoting right in front of the dog. If they got up, it was a pretty simple matter to correct them and put them back in the stay. As the dogs got used to doing the stay like this, we either lengthened the time we did the stay or moved farther and farther back from the dog, but we never increased length of time and distance at the same time.

While sometimes Olaf would get it and do the stay just fine, other times he acted bored and got up and walked toward me. I was at a loss as to why he would do it great one time and then not another. Usually, sit-stays or down-stays were at the end of class, and that was when I began to notice that Olaf had reached the end of his attention span. So now the trick was to work with him at home every day doing sit-stays, down-stays and coming when called—or, in Olaf and Skylar's case, when the "come" hand signal was given.

Gradually, Olaf became better at sit-stays and recalls, but I usually had to do things to keep his attention on me; otherwise, he was busy looking around, and when it came time for me to give the hand signal to come, he was oftentimes checking out his fellow students in class. I ended up using a hand signal with my arm fully extended and my hand up in a "stop" position all the while he was doing a stay. This is allowed to take the TDI test, so I practiced with my arm outstretched with my hand up every time we decided to work on sit-stays or down-stays. Eventually, he got it and just in time to take the TDI test.

I also wanted to test Olaf and Skylar together so that I could take them together on visits. My thought was that, since people are already fascinated by Skylar being deaf, how wonderful it would be if two deaf dogs were to make visits and prove their worth as therapy dogs. I was unsure how much of the test I would have to take with both Olaf and Skylar. I emailed our evaluator, Tim, and he said that we had to do the whole test together, including the group sit/stay and down/stay but not the recall. To say the least, I was horrified that I would have to go through the group sit/stay and down/stay with both of the dogs. I started thinking that maybe I wouldn't test them together yet—get Olaf tested this year, and work on testing them together next year.

But then, I thought about what my goals, my life's purpose, are, and visiting with these two hearing-impaired dogs and bringing joy into people's lives gave me a renewed sense of purpose. I started training with both Sky and Olaf in my basement, walking on a loose leash together, performing sit/stays and down/stays. Yes, it was difficult at times. I hadn't worked with Skylar on obedience issues for a year. While I know she hadn't forgotten anything, she was really rusty on doing downs and stays. So we started working every day together—the three of us—down in the basement, walking in circles, halting so they would learn to sit when I stopped, sitting and staying and performing a down and staying. Each day they got a little better at performing the tasks. I made sure to end each session on a positive note with lots of treats and hugs for each one of them.

The handler is not allowed to use treats when taking the TDI test. That caused me some consternation because I was very good at lavishing treats on any dog I'm training—especially if they are a food-oriented dog. Some dogs respond well to a pat of the head and a "good dog" shout-out from the handler. Since Olaf and Sky can't hear me tell them what good dogs they are, I found it easier to give them treats when they do a task correctly. And in particular, Skylar shies away from any hand looming over her head to give her a pat. Some dogs are "head shy" that way. I found the answer for testing these two without treats was to run through some of the test elements outside away from the facility, and I give them lots of treats. Then I come into the building and do the test. The dog still thinks they are going to get a treat, and by the time they've figured out that they aren't getting any treats, the test is over. I know, that sounds underhanded and shady, but it has worked in the past for a couple of my dogs that are food-oriented only, not toy-oriented or praise-oriented.

Saturday, December 19, 2015, dawned cold, but sunny. We had had quite a stretch of gray, warm (for Minnesota) and drizzly weather through November and December. But the sun being out on the nineteenth seemed to help my attitude. I hooked up both Skylar and Olaf, and we drove over to EZ Obedience for the test. I was extremely worried because Olaf was acting like a madman when I hooked up the leash, running in circles and barking at everything that moved. I honestly thought that we would fail the test because he was so full of "pee and vinegar," and I was afraid he wouldn't be able to settle down.

When we got to the facility, I put Skylar in a crate to wait and see if Olaf and I passed first before we tried testing together. The beginning part of the test required those people testing to sit at a table with their dog and fill out the required paperwork for TDI while the dog sits quietly at their side. Olaf was so excited to see everyone, and though his ears don't fully function, his nose is in tip-top condition. He could smell all the wonderful baked goods that people had brought for those testing and because it was close to Christmastime. I kept trying to keep him quiet while I filled out my paperwork, but for the most part, Olaf wasn't having any of it.

I really wanted to test toward the beginning because I wanted to know if Olaf passed, then Sky, Olaf, and I could take the test together. As it turned out though, we were the last team to test. There were seven teams that tested that day, and seven teams passed. Tim is a great evaluator—he can just tell which teams will make good therapy teams—and it's not necessarily the teams that are perfect in obedience.

Olaf was still very distracted by the time we tested, and I found myself yanking on his leash to get him to pay attention to me. Tim corrected me several times and had me do some of the maneuvers twice—without pulling on Olaf. I was honestly so nervous about passing the test that I know my nervousness translated all the way down the leash to Olaf. We made it through the test, and Tim passed us and not because we tested very well but because he knew that my dogs and I make good therapy teams and that I needed to relax on the leash when visiting with Olaf. Phew, one down, one to go.

I took Skylar out of the crate, and together the three of us tested. We had to walk through the crowd, make a visit, do a down-stay and a few of the other parts of the test. The test with Sky and Olaf together though was very short and abbreviated. Tim was interested in how well we worked as a threesome. Thank the Lord, the three of us passed, so we were now on our way to fulfilling my life's purpose—making visits with my deaf shelties and advocating for them all the while bringing happiness to others. We were on a roll. And I'm proud to say that Skylar and Olaf are the first deaf therapy dog team passed by TDI. It just doesn't get any better than this!

CHAPTER FIFTEEN

MacPherson

I had been feeling very lonely since having to send Mario to the Rainbow Bridge. Several friends suggested that I get a puppy to fill the void—no, no more puppies. But I would consider adopting an older dog if the right one came along. Darn that Facebook. I spend entirely too much time on Facebook seeing all the different rescues' posts about dogs available for adoption. One post on the Central Illinois Sheltie Rescue Facebook page caught my eye. It was of a sable-and-white sheltie named Misha, who was deaf. They had posted a video on their page, showing his foster mom training him on the basics like sit, down, stay, and come. Misha looked a lot like Skylar with a split face with one blue eye and one brown eye. And from the video, I could tell this little guy was smart and was picking up the hand cues very quickly.

I messaged the rescue and asked if they adopted outside Illinois. They said they did but that I needed to fill out an application form for them to consider me. So I did, and they got back to me pretty quickly and said that, yes, they would be willing to adopt Misha to me. There was one catch though—they wanted me to go there so they could meet me and pick up the dog. I'm not the best winter driver, and the older I get, the more I dislike driving in the winter. Making an eight-hundred-mile round-trip just didn't excite me at all, but I said that I would leave on January 1, drive down there, stay overnight, and then pick up Misha in the morning and then head back. I arranged for a pet sitter for one night for my fur kids at home.

One of my bookkeeping clients at the time, Juli, asked if I had any plans for a vacation. I told her that with all my dogs, vacations really weren't an option and that I actually enjoyed being home with my dogs more than traveling. Yes, I have definitely become an old fogie. But I told her that I was taking a drive trip down to Bloomington, Illinois, to pick up a dog and then coming back. Juli is a pilot and owns her own plane. She offered to fly me down there, pick up the dog, have lunch, and fly back home and be back by four o'clock. How could I resist an offer like that?

I offered to pay all the gas, and she said I needed to pay the gas for one way and she would pick up the other because it gave her more hours of flying time. Juli owns a landscape business and had a new grandson, and being busy running the business and enjoying her new grandson had kept her from flying much in the summer and fall of 2015. The offer was too good to be true. We set it for January 2, 2016, to fly down there. And of course, everything depended on the weather. As the first crept closer, I kept watching the forecast—not only for the Twin Cities area but also for Iowa and Illinois also.

Juli and I connected on January 1, and Juli decided it was a go for the next day as the forecast was for cold but clear skies. It looked like it would be a perfect day for flying. Bright and early on January 2, I picked up my friend Celeste, who was flying down with us, and we drove out to the airport. Celeste's husband, Rob, came along and took pictures of us by Juli's plane and as we were in the air, taking off. It was a perfect day to fly, and Juli is a wonderfully skilled pilot.

The feeling of peace while flying was undeniable. While it was noisy in the sense that we each had to wear headphones to hear one another, it was still incredibly peaceful looking down on cities and farm fields that I had seen only from my 5'7" perspective on the ground. I could see where becoming a pilot and enjoying the views of verdant fields or even snow-covered lakes as we saw could become addictive.

We got into Bloomington, Illinois, in two hours, and Juli's landing was so smooth that none of us even felt the plane touch down.

We decided to have lunch in the airport, and after lunch, Natalie, from the Central Illinois Sheltie Rescue, would pick us up, drive us to her place, about fifteen minutes away, and pick up Misha. Off we went to Natalie's home. Misha was enclosed in the kitchen area, so I could have a good look at him and see if I really wanted to adopt him. How could I not want him? He is a dog so full of joy with life and people that he can barely contain it. He is bigger than Skylar and Olaf, who are themselves bigger than the average sheltie standard. I guess the "lethal white" gene and the "merle" gene do produce bigger dogs.

My bond with him was instantaneous. His foster parents were there, and they scrutinized me to be sure than Misha/MacPherson (as I ended up calling him) would be a good match for me. They decided that they liked me, so I completed all the adoption paperwork, wrote out the check, and Mac's foster parents gave us a ride back to the airport so we could take off for Minnesota.

What an adventure. We had placed a collapsible canvas crate in the back area of Juli's plane. However, after being airborne only twenty minutes, Mac wanted out of the crate and wanted to sit on my lap. I unzipped the crate and let him climb into my lap, where he sat the whole rest of the way home. We were facing a headwind going back to Minnesota, so Juli warned me to keep a grip on him as there might be some turbulence, but thankfully, we didn't encounter any problems and made it back to Hutchinson, Minnesota, about 4:30 p.m. Celeste and I helped roll Juli's plane back into the hangar. I gave Juli a big hug and a thank-you for flying Mac to Minnesota, and headed home to begin introducing Mac into his new pack.

Dusk was setting in by the time I got home, so I drove Mac and me into the garage and then let him run around the backyard to do his business and smell as many smells as he could before I let the rest of the pack out. For some reason, I was thinking that there might be a confrontation between Olaf and Mac, but everyone got along fine. Honestly, I have found this to be such an easy way to introduce a new dog to my pack, and I'm so grateful that I seem to have a pretty well-balanced pack. Sure, there are squabbles here and there, and one of the more dominant dogs has to put someone in their place.

But I have not had any outright dog fights in my pack, and I am so thankful for that.

Obedience training didn't begin until the third week of February, so I decided to let Mac get used to his new environment. Mack settled in with playing with all the dogs but, in particular, Olaf and Skylar. I don't know if because all three are deaf and they get their communication signals from their other senses, but the three "deafies" hang together and play together all the time. Maybe it's because all three are fairly young. Who knows? All I do know is that all three love to play together both outside and inside.

One thing I noticed right away with MacPherson is that he seems to be fairly needy. What I mean by that is that, when I lie down on the bed, he has to jump up and be right next to me, often putting half of his body on mine. There are times when that is very endearing, but there are other times when it's not so fun having the weight of a dog on you. It sounds like he was left alone a lot in his former home, and I knew that all he wanted was to be fed and to be loved. I knew I could fulfill those two needs in his life, and I let him lie next to me or at least put his head on my lap or chest whenever he felt the need. Obviously, he has a lot more confidence now, and only occasionally does he want to put his head on my shoulder or lap. The majority of the time, he'll lie right next to me on the bed or down by my feet. He's getting braver and braver all the time, and it does my heart good to know that he is feeling more confident.

The Monday before we started our obedience training, I decided to take Mac for a little walk to a friend's house. I hadn't had him on leash since I brought him home—partly because the sidewalks were very icy this winter and I didn't want to take a chance on falling and possibly breaking an ankle. When I hooked up Mac's leash, he became a madman. He was so excited that he kept jumping up on me and spinning circles. Once we started walking, he wanted to be three feet ahead of me, sniffing everything he could sniff and still be in front of me. Right away I knew that loose leash training was going to be what we needed to work on most in beginning obedience. When I gave him the traditional signal for heel (left arm straight at my side and then swing the arm up and bend at the elbow), Mac took the signal as it was time to run and race. Yikes, we have a lot of work to do.

Our first night of class found Mac super excited at first, but once all the other trainees and their dogs filed in, he started to cling to me more. All we did the first night were heel and sit and sit-stays standing right in front of the dog. I was so impressed with how well Mac did, considering there were a total of eleven teams training that evening. Thank heavens, Mac loves treats as he is more than willing to work when there is a goodie involved at the end of it.

The third week of class, we start doing the "heel" down game. At the end of class, the group is given commands like heel, halt (sit), circle right or left, about face, come forth, among others. The last dog to do the command correctly is eliminated. I admit I'm fairly competitive. I had done really well with Olaf in the heel-down game, and I expected Mackie P to do the same. Was I in for a surprise.

The trainer called out various commands, and Mackie was doing great. Then when he called out "Halt," Mackie sat, but he sat perpendicular to me instead of parallel, and we ended up being the first ones eliminated. I was frustrated—heck I wanted to win the heel-down game, but Mackie was not complying.

I posted a picture of Mac on Facebook and explained what he was doing. Quite a few people replied that their dogs always sat crooked or somewhat facing them also. Kelli, one of the therapy dog teams in our chapter, suggested that when we were heeling clockwise, to hug the wall so that Mac had to sit straight. He had no room to sit perpendicular.

The next week I tried it with Mac. Kelli was right—he sat straight alongside me whenever we were heeling clockwise. Now the problem was getting him to sit straight when we were heeling counterclockwise and had no wall to hug. We were eliminated second this time. I felt frustrated, but Chucki, one of the other trainers, asked me why I cared if he sat straight or not. I had no intentions of taking him into obedience trials as I planned for him to be another one of my therapy dogs. The dog only has to sit to pass the therapy test. Correct form is not a requirement for the TDI test.

Chucki also made an astute observation from watching Mackie and me perform various obedience tasks from the sidelines. She noted that, when he sits crooked, he is always looking at my face, as if he's trying to observe what my reaction or even emotion is at the time. Duh! I can't believe how dense I am that I didn't catch on to the fact that he's deaf and he wants to watch me for signs and signals that he's doing things right. This is what I've wanted from my deaf dogs—for them to keep their eyes on me so I can give them the thumbs-up, a treat, or the next hand signal. So thank you, Chucki, for helping me to understand why Mackie sits crooked!

We finished up our first round of Beginning Obedience classes together. Mackie still sits crooked and stares at me, but he sits every time I ask. He tends to forge ahead and seems to have the most difficulty of walking on a loose leash of my three deaf shelties. But we have many months to work on it before we start taking the therapy dog classes.

The Minnesota Sheltie Rescue holds its annual reunion in April of each year. Anyone who has adopted a sheltie from the rescue or who has fostered a sheltie or has volunteered or transported dogs is welcome to come with their dog(s). This year I decided to bring my three little "deafies" as I call them.

The previous week I had attended the Dog Olympics at the Minnesota State Fairgrounds. I took Harley along to help work the Minnesota Wisconsin Collie Rescue booth. Another volunteer, Doug, was also helping in the booth along with Terry, the president of the rescue. As it became time for me to leave, Terry mentioned that she was helping out at the sheltie reunion the following week. She asked me if I was going and I told her that I was planning on bringing the three deafies. Doug asked if he could come along to give me help at the reunion. Of course I said yes.

Doug and I arrived at the reunion site at about the same time. Initially I gave him Skylar to work with since she's fairly quiet and compliant. I dealt with Olaf and MacPherson. We had barely gotten our registration information in hand when a friend from the sheltie rescue came up to talk and say hi. Mackie was so excited to see her that he could barely contain himself.

PJ had had a rough year both emotionally and physically. She had lost her two shelties to her ex-husband in a divorce, so she was really looking forward to getting some therapy from the shelties at the reunion. Little did I know that PJ was instrumental in getting Mackie into rescue for the Central Illinois Sheltie Rescue. The fact that he remembered her and was leaping about and jumping up on her in excitement really did my heart good.

PJ had driven up all the way from Iowa when Domino went missing to help search for him. PJ and her then husband had fostered Domi until they moved and were unable to foster him. They felt so bad about his escape that they spent a whole afternoon with me searching for him. PJ is a wonderful, caring dog lover, and I was so grateful for her help in trying to find Domino.

Mackie was so enamored with seeing PJ again that the two took off together to visit the various booths at the reunion and head outside for Mackie to do his business. It's amazing how God's plan works. PJ and I had been friends on Facebook since 2011 and had messaged back and forth, but I had no idea she was the one to get Mackie into rescue. So here I was with two dogs in my life that PJ had had a hand in helping get to me. I'm so glad that she was able to spend time with Mackie and get all sorts of kisses and affection from him. I know it did her a world of good to break away from the medical testing and get some pet therapy from a dog she helped get into rescue.

Meanwhile, Doug and I were working with Olaf and Skylar and having a good time of it. Toward the end of the reunion, Doug mentioned to me that he was really impressed with my deaf shelties. He really wanted a collie but had wanted to come and check out shelties. He knew them to be more hyper than collies, which is a fact. But Skylar, Olaf, and Mackie had been on their best behavior all afternoon and he was so impressed by them that he made the decision to adopt a deaf sheltie if one should become available. He asked for my help if he should need it, and I gladly said anytime. My heart was soaring that I wasn't the only person enamored with my deaf shelties. It was a fantastic day and I drove home with a huge smile on my face.

And my three deafies were so tuckered out that they slept the whole way home.

Mackie and I went through a second round of Beginning Obedience. Mackie did great with sitting, down, stay, and come when signaled. I was anxious to take the therapy dog classes, which started the week after we finished the obedience classes. The only problem was that they were held on a night when I work. I wouldn't be able to attend any of the classes, and that bummed me out immensely. We exposed Mackie to wheelchairs, walkers, canes, etc., when our therapy dog chapter had a meeting. He seemed to have no problems with the equipment. All I could do was pray that he would do well at the test.

The week before the TDI test, I found out that the test itself had changed. I had already tested and passed with five other dogs, and there was one change in the six years since I first started testing my dogs with TDI. I quickly got on the TDI website and printed out the test. I was really nervous about the part where we make a visit. I knew he would be great at making a visit because he truly loves people, but the visitor was supposed to offer the dog a treat, and we were supposed to tell the dog "No, leave it" I had never practiced this with Mackie—in fact, I didn't even have a hand signal for "Leave it." I was panicking because Mackie is a dog who will take the treat from your hand along with a couple of your fingers.

The night before the TDI test, I attended a Christmas party at the house of one of my bookkeeping clients. While at the party, I could tell that I was coming down with a cold—scratchy throat, achy body, headache—all the symptoms of a cold. I didn't sleep at all that night. I don't know if I was just nervous about taking the test or if the cold symptoms were keeping me from sleeping, but I ended up with only two hours of sleep.

Saturday, December 10, 2016, dawned cold, but no snow was predicted until later in the day. I forced myself to get up and take Mackie for a walk before we drove over to take the test. Mackie has a ton of energy, and I wanted him to use some of it up on our walk. Once back from the walk, I brushed him up and practiced a bit in the basement on long sits, downs, and recalls from a distance. He was doing everything correctly.

God must have been smiling on me as we took the test. Mackie did everything great. I was the one that was making mistakes. I don't know if it was the lack of sleep, the cold whose symptoms were full blown by the test, or nervousness about the new test, but I was probably more "heavy-handed" with the leash than I should have been. Hooray, Tim passed us, and I know it wasn't because of my stellar performance. He has been the evaluator for my other dogs, and he knows how I am on therapy dog visits. Mackie is the sixth dog of mine that has passed the TDI test, and he is now my fourth active therapy dog. Needless to say, I promptly sent off his registration papers, health paperwork, and my money to TDI. I'm anxious to get back his credentials so we can start making visits. Mackie is going to make a wonderful therapy dog. His love for humans knows no bounds, and his enthusiasm eclipses the love he shows. I'm also going to teach him a few tricks to entertain the people that we visit. Ah, another goal reached all because of a loving, deaf rescue dog! I am so lucky!

CHAPTER SIXTEEN

Visits from Angels in a Dog Suit (And Beyond Basic Therapy Visits)

There are so many places to visit with your therapy dog to bring some joy into people's lives. Let me tell you about my experiences at different facilities—experiences that are both good and bad.

Most people are familiar with therapy visits where you bring the dogs into a nursing home facility and visit with the residents and allow them to pet the dogs. I started out my therapy team life doing basic visits like that. Nursing homes and assisted-living centers are very similar, so let's talk about them. Before I have visited any facility, I call and talk to the activities director or volunteer coordinator, whoever handles volunteers coming into that facility. I explain to the coordinator about how the dogs are all tested and registered with one of the national registering organizations. As part of being registered, each dog has to make a visit to the veterinarian once a year, make sure their shots are updated, are in general good health, and that we are provided with a liability insurance policy. I also explain that our dogs are there to give comfort and for people to touch and pet. Once the coordinator understands all these things, we find a date that works for both the facility and for me (or the members of our chapter).

Our group has found it best to meet outside the facility or, if it's wintertime, just inside the door before we go in to meet the residents of any given facility. Our group had an incident where two members were making a visit to a long-term care facility. The mother-in-law of one of the teams lived at this facility, and she was really looking forward to the visit. The team with the mother-in-law in residence arrived first and went into the facility. Her mother-in-law saw her with the dog and came over to pet the dog. She was standing behind the dog at this time. The second team entered the facility, and both dogs made movements to get to each other and greet and play. Unfortunately, the first dog backed up (in dog play) and knocked the handler's mother-in-law over. She ended up breaking her ankle and had to be taken to the hospital. Unfortunately, the team member felt so bad about what happened to her mother-in-law that she stopped making visits. As a way to circumvent incidents like this from happening in the future, we have made it a rule that all team members making a visit will meet outside the facility or just inside the door so that the dogs can greet each other and get all their greetings to each other over with before we start our visit.

I have made visits to facilities where I had wonderful experiences and I've made visits where I came home and wondered why I had made the visit. Our group has made visits at facilities where no one had a clue that we were going to visit even though we had a standing date to come or had just talked to the coordinator a couple of days before. We stopped going to several facilities for that reason. We are all volunteers, and while we absolutely love bringing our dogs in to visit people, our time is precious too. The goal for a visit is to come home feeling exhilarated knowing you might have made a small difference in someone's life even if only for a moment. But to be made to feel like we're not welcome or that maybe we've intruded on another activity going on doesn't sit very well with me.

We had one nursing home facility that didn't really understand the reasons for our visits. Instead of bringing people out into the main living area that wanted to interact with the dogs, there were quite a few people that had no interest in seeing the dogs or even having the dogs near to them. After the group experienced this several visits in a row, the teams became frustrated and decided not to schedule any more visits. Two years passed before we tried again. In that time, the facility had hired a new activities director, and that made all the difference. She put all those residents who wanted to interact with the dogs in a separate room where we could visit with them and not interfere with those that had no interest in seeing the dogs. That made all the difference, and the visits have been great ever since.

I have found that the volunteer or activities coordinator at each facility we visit can make or break our visit experience. It's imperative to be in contact with the coordinator a day before to ensure they are expecting the therapy teams.

My very first visit with Mario was at a nursing home facility in Arizona. They had arranged the residents in a semicircle, and we brought the dogs in, introduced ourselves, and talked a little bit about our dogs. After the introductions, we went around the circle, bringing the dogs close for the residents to pet. One of the dementia patients at the home was pulling a little too energetically on Mario's soft, furry coat, and it was then that I realized that I needed to be the advocate for my dog. Safety of the people we visit and being my dog's advocate are the number one priorities on any visit. I had to pry the patient's hand off Mario, and she took it in stride. But I learned that on any visit, I need to be right there with my dog with my hand on his or her collar in case I needed to pull the dog away quickly from the situation. But hey, I was learning new tricks all in my first visit.

I have made many visits to nursing homes and assisted-living centers over my ten-year "career" as a therapy team. I remember one visit to a long term care facility in Glencoe, Minnesota. I had brought Harley with on this visit. People are usually fascinated by his gleaming white coat and his blue merle-colored head. However, Harley brought with him his one trait that has me frustrated. He is constantly "talking." It's not a bark, it's not a whine, but it's something like he's trying to talk. Now I know he probably does have a lot to say, but patients, children, anyone with normal hearing find Harley's talking irritating. I kept trying to get Harley not to talk on the visit, but he just kept voicing his opinion on things. It got to the point that I had to walk outside with Harley because the talking was disturbing to the residents. I have not figured out yet how to keep Harley quiet on visits, so I don't use him for visits into nursing homes or schools for reading programs because I can't keep him quiet. Instead I use him for obedience demonstrations, for square dancing (I'll talk about this later), and for doing drill maneuvers. For some reason, he doesn't find it necessary to talk during these activities.

Visits to nursing homes and assisted-living facilities make up the bulk of my therapy dog visits. It's always gratifying to strike up a conversation with a lonely older person. They love talking about the dogs in their past. Being that Hutchinson is mostly an agricultural community, many of the residents of the local nursing homes are former farmers. They relish talking about their experiences with their working farm dogs—whether they were collies, German shepherds, or mixed breed—they always delight in talking about their former four-legged friends and how they herded cows, sheep, ducks or just stood guard on the farm. I love visits like these where these gentle old people have such rich histories and like to share them with those of us visiting.

Hospitals—when I started making therapy visits, I did a lot of hospital work. I found good and bad about visiting at hospitals. First off, they do have a lot of rules and regulations, and you have to comply with them or you can't make visits. There were some hospital visits I made where every door I knocked on wanted a visit from the dogs. But there were also visits where very few to none wanted a visit or they may have been sleeping or being monitored by hospital staff. Since moving back to Minnesota, I have made no hospital visits. The local hospital has very few rooms with few patients staying there. If I lived in a bigger town, I would probably consider making hospital visits again. I always felt that many of the therapy visits were for the employees and staff. They always get excited seeing the dogs, and being able to give them a break from their difficult jobs made me feel good.

I was recently reminded by my friend Kit about a funny incident that happened at the hospital in Kingman. Kit and Doodle had gone in to visit patients one day, but the minute she got in the door, the volunteer coordinator very sternly told her to go to her office immediately. Kit and Doodle followed her to her office. It appears that one of the doctors had reported a "brown mess" in the hallway near the hospital pharmacy. The reporting doctor had been opposed to having the dogs come into the hospital, and he was probably hopeful that this incident would signal the end of the therapy dog program in the hospital.

Kit explained that she had just arrived at the hospital and wasn't aware of any other teams coming to the hospital that day. Kit and the coordinator walked over to where the offending "brown mess" was. By this time, the hospital cleaning people all dressed in hazmat suits were in the process of cleaning up the "brown mess." Any idea what the offending mess was? It turns out it was prunes that someone had dropped. Kit burst out laughing at the sight of the cleaning crew all dressed up in hazmat suits, picking up prunes. Needless to say, the volunteer coordinator apologized to Kit for the assumptions made. This incident was a good reminder to all of us though that accidents can happen, and it's incumbent on the dog handler to report any mess made by their dog and get the cleaning people there immediately to make sure the area has been sterilized sufficiently. It's also a good lesson that, while some people in authority may oppose having dogs visit in a hospital setting, persevere through all the negativity by showing the positive effects of pet therapy visits—lowering patient blood pressure, putting a smile on a patient's face by petting a dog's silky fur, and allowing patients to forget for a while why they are in the hospital in the first place and what's happening to their bodies. The positive effects have been documented over and over and far outweigh the negatives of having dogs in a hospital setting. It turns out that the reporting doctor asked Kit one day to really explain the purpose of therapy dog visits. Once she had enumerated all the positive effects, he finally agreed that the positive effects on patients could be measured in the more positive outlook on patients who had received dog visits. Another victory for Kit—way to go!

Schools and colleges—making visits to schools are some of my favorite events. Allowing children to read to the dogs is very satisfying. Kids love to read to the dogs. There is no peer pressure, and they are put more at ease by petting the dog at the same time they are reading to them. The READ program focuses on reaching children before third grade to help improve their reading. The child reads to the dog, and it's up to the handler to ask questions of the child to see if they are comprehending what they are reading. These questions can be asked using the dog such as "What do you think Olaf thinks happened?" Having kids read to my therapy dogs has always been very gratifying for me.

The READ© program was designed for children that are having trouble with their reading skills. It's a great program, but I have often felt sad for the other kids in the classroom because seeing the dogs can be beneficial for them also. My friend Kit and I developed basic math questions to be used for the children not in the reading program. A couple of sample questions include "Olaf's tail is ten inches long, and Harley's tail is sixteen inches long. If you laid their two tails end to end, how many inches would they stretch?" Another example of a math question: "Doodle gets a bath every time before he makes a therapy visit. Doodle makes two therapy visits a week. How many baths in a year does Doodle have?" These are just samples of questions you can ask. Kids seem to enjoy these questions because they can see the dogs right in front of them and therefore relate to the questions a little more than they can to the typical math problem.

Another area of pet therapy visits that has taken off in recent years is to bring therapy dogs onto college and university campuses during semester finals. The students are under a lot of pressure studying and cramming to take finals, and petting the dogs before taking a test can ease the tension they are feeling, lower their blood pressure, and provide a sense of calm. Bringing therapy dogs is catching on throughout the country, and it's really helping students. Just another way dogs can enrich the lives of all people.

Libraries—libraries, like schools, often have READ© program for the kids to read to the dogs. I have attended a couple of visits at the Litchfield Library for preschool kids. The children's librarian has all the kids and the therapy dog teams sit in a circle. She plays a guitar, and we sing several songs with the kids. Each of the teams introduces themselves and their dog. Then the kids are allowed to ask questions and pick a book that they would like the therapy dog team to read to them. These are fun visits, and the kids learn not to be scared of dogs at an early age. The parents are with their little ones, and the kids are taught to ask if they can pet the dogs. All in all, these are very satisfying visits.

Veterans hospitals—when I first moved back to Minnesota, I wanted to visit at the Minneapolis Veterans Hospital with Mario. When I finally reached the person who could help me with that, she let me know that they already had a group from another registering organization that visited with their dogs. They were very strict on the visits and had a waiting list of potential visiting teams. I never was able to make a visit to the Minneapolis Veterans Hospital, but I know of other teams that do visit there and they have had great visits with the vets.

Veterans homes—in early 2015, my eighty-eight-year-old dad found that he had to move out of his co-op apartment because of a raise in the rent. My sister and I worked very hard to get him admitted into the Minneapolis Veterans Home. To our face, Dad acted as if he were all in for moving to the Veterans Home. Dad grew up less than a mile away from the Veterans Home, and back when he grew up, it was called "the old soldiers home," and it was not a place that you wanted to send your aging parents. It was shabby, in disrepair, and poorly managed. I know that Dad carried these memories of "the old soldiers home" inside and wasn't very happy to have to share a room with someone. On my birthday in early April, my sister and I took Dad to the Veterans Home for his interview. He aced the interview and stated he couldn't wait to move in so that he could help other veterans do things. I was so proud of Dad after this interview because he was thinking of others. However, a different outcome was in store for Dad.

Dad's birthday was less than a week from mine, and my sister and I had plans to take him out for lunch to celebrate his eighty-ninth birthday. We received a call early the morning of his birthday from the manager of the coop where he lived that he had passed away in his sleep. Both my sister and I were numb with shock. While we knew his health had been going downhill and that he needed more care than he was getting at his apartment, we were still in shock. Add to that the shock we received when we rushed over to Dad's apartment complex and talked to his friends and buddies. All of them said that Dad did not want to move to the Veterans Home, but he didn't tell us that little tidbit of information because he didn't want to put more stress on us trying to find him a place to live that he could afford.

I spent the rest of 2015 and up until the time of this writing in 2016 missing my dad. I had planned to bring Harley and the "deafies" over to the Veterans Home for visits. My dad loved dogs so much, and he was so excited that I would be bringing the dogs over to help brighten his day and also other veterans in the facility. I've spent many a night sobbing over the loss of my parents, and I've spent more times than I care to count feeling adrift without that solid family anchor I had always relied on. But I also know that Dad left this world not having to move to the Veterans Home, a place he really didn't want to move. And when I find myself having a crying jag, I just lie down on the bed and allow however many of my dogs want to come up and lie down with me. If I'm crying, I usually have at least three that lie right next to me with their heads on my legs or chest. They always work their therapy on me!

Another Veteran's facility that I visited with another team member was the Eagle's Healing Nest. It is a facility for veterans suffering from PTSD. I was so excited to make this visit because I know that therapy dogs can make such a difference in veterans with PTSD. I called and talked to one of the administrators of the facility, and we arranged a date on a Saturday for us to visit.

Bright and early, I set off with Skylar to the facility. It was easily a two-and-a-half-hour drive away from my home, but the day was beautiful and I hadn't been on a drive anywhere for quite a while. The drive up was uneventful, and when I arrived on the grounds of the facility, I was amazed at how beautiful the setting was. In its former incarnation, it was a girl's reformatory. The early 1900s structures were beautiful, and these stately old buildings were on a generous pastoral acreage. Once my other teammate and I made it up there, we went up to the administration building to check in and find out where we would be visiting with the vets. I had expected to see some of the vets sitting in a room where we could bring our dogs to them for some interaction and conversation. Instead the administrator said that we could go visit the vets in the residence halls. There were three residence halls at that time. One of them they called "the cat house" because the men living there had cats as pets. So we were down to two halls that we could visit. The administrator also happened to mention that several of the vets were training their own therapy dogs. I thought that was a fantastic idea until we started visiting the two "non-cat" halls.

We walked into the first residence hall, expecting to find some of the men sitting around. We didn't see anyone. We started walking down one of the residence halls and checking in the rooms to see if anyone wanted a visit. We only saw two men, and neither wanted a therapy dog visit. However, we did see one German shepherd who came out to greet us. He was being trained by one of the vets as his PTSD therapy dog. The dog was friendly, and his owner was willing to talk to us. After several minutes of conversation, we decided to try the other residence hall.

We walked up to the big entry door and since I was in the lead, I opened the door and walked in with Skylar. There were no humans about, but from around the corner came three big pit bulls racing up to us at full speed. I have nothing against pit bulls, but any encounter between a dog on a leash and a dog off leash is decidedly not in favor of the dog on a leash. Diane, who was right behind me, was very uncomfortable. No one came to get the dogs—nothing. I said to Diane to just slowly back out the door, which we did. Neither Rudy nor Skylar was hurt, and I'm not saying the pit bulls would have caused trouble, but I will not put my dog at risk in a situation where my dog is on leash and the "dog of the house" is off leash.

After we got outside with our two dogs safely, we stopped to talk about the visit and make comments. I felt that I had let both Diane and myself down. I was the one who had set up the visit, but I obviously had not made clear what I expected from the visit—that being the vets who wanted interaction with therapy dogs in a central area without other dogs present. Since the facility was so far from home, we decided that visiting there was not in the best interest of the therapy dogs. I do believe in the power of therapy dogs though, and I'm thrilled that many of the veterans in the facility are training their own dogs, forming special bonds with their dogs, and experiencing the unconditional love that only dogs can give.

Funeral homes—visiting at funeral homes is a fairly new phenomenon. I can honestly say that, when my dad passed away in 2015 and our first stop was the funeral home where my parents had purchased cremation policies decades before, it would have been so comforting to have a dog to pet and sink my fingers into their fur. But this facility did not have comfort or therapy dogs, so my sister and I were left to deal with a funeral for Dad and facing sticker shock at how much costs had increased since my parents had purchased their policies.

I have not explored visiting our local funeral home yet or even if they would be interested in having a therapy dog there. To me the best time for a therapy dog visit is when the family is planning the funeral. They are often in shock and grief and having a warm body of fur to pet can bring some respite of comfort.

Courts—when I lived in Arizona, I worked for the Superior Court. I daily saw the kids going for court hearings, and I noticed the scared looks on their faces. Through the CASA (Court Appointed Special Advocate) program, therapy dogs were allowed into the courthouse before court proceedings for kids to pet before court hearings. Therapy dogs were allowed access after I moved back to Minnesota. I think it's an excellent program and a great way for dogs to work their special magic on children. Our county court is located in another town, and we have no CASA services here. Several of us have been trying to get permission to bring our dogs in but so far have been met with resistance. Often, privacy concerns are noted—especially since we live in a less populated county. However, we are still trying to make headway into helping kids through the court system.

Airports—bringing therapy dogs into airports is an idea that has caught on in some of the major airports in the US. The Minneapolis airport has a therapy dog pool of teams on the premises—especially for those busy travel days at Thanksgiving and Christmas. When storms delay and cancel flights, it's nice to have a therapy dog to pet to calm your nerves. I personally have not signed up for doing this yet because of the drive, but it's something I've been considering doing with my therapy dogs.

Rehabilitation facilities—there is an offshoot of therapy dog visits called Animal Assisted Therapy, where a therapy dog team works with one patient and one patient caregiver to help the patient in their rehabilitation. Pet Partners is the only registering organization that tests and registers Animal Assisted Therapy teams. Often these teams are paid for their services; otherwise, all other therapy visits are made on a volunteer only basis. My dogs and I have never done official Animal Assisted Therapy although, when I lived in Arizona, when we visited the hospital, we saved visiting the rehab unit last. There were several patients on the unit when we would visit, and many of them were trying to strengthen arm movements, hand movements, and even walking unassisted. The rehab unit welcomed help from our dogs by allowing patients to throw balls for the dogs that they would retrieve then take the ball from the dog's mouth. Also, bigger dogs were sometimes used to help facilitate someone trying to walk without a walker by using a cane and having the dog on the other side to lean on if needed. Visiting the rehab units always made my visits complete. It was so good to see people making physical strides and being so grateful for the help of the therapy dogs.

Hospice facilities—I have covered my experiences with hospice earlier. However, I'm happy to say that there is another hospice service in Hutchinson that wants therapy teams to make visits in Winthrop, Hutchinson, and Glencoe. This service does not have the same requirements as Allina had, such as forcing the handler to have a flu shot and filling out forms regarding the patient's emotional state. Rather they are more concerned that any of their hospice patients are not in pain, and we have to fill out forms to that effect. Did the patient seem in pain, moaning, crying? They are most concerned that the patients in their care are not in pain and I absolutely concur with that. As of this writing, four of our teams are going to be going through the hospice training, including me, and will start making visits as soon as everything is completed. Again, many of the hospice visits I made in the past were about giving the family of the hospice patient some pet therapy. I can't wait to get started on making hospice visits again.

Veterans groups such as the American Legion and VFW—four of our therapy dog teams made a visit to the American Legion group in 2015. We attended one of their dinner meetings and explained what our dogs do and the purpose for therapy dogs. I was so impressed with the dogs because there was some very good-smelling food and none of the dogs acted up and tried to get to the food. The vets asked some great questions, and we were happy to answer all of them. After our visit was over, the veterans gave us a hand and thanked us profusely for bringing in the dogs to brighten their evening.

Alzheimer's facilities—several of the nursing homes we visit have Alzheimer's units contained within the home. Every month our group makes a visit to Harmony River, and each month we visit the Alzheimer's unit. These people are always happy to see the dogs. Often we have to help them to pet the dogs by taking their hand and helping them to stroke the dog's fur. Those that are still verbal will often bring up dogs in their past, indicating that we are reaching them on some level. And of course we make time to visit with the staff so they can get a little pet therapy themselves. Working with Alzheimer's patients is a difficult and stressful job, and anything we can do to help the staff out is very appreciated.

Domestic violence safe house and facilities—this is an area that I have tried to break into while living in Hutchinson. The local group that serves victims of domestic violence does not have a facility where these victims are housed. Rather they are scattered throughout the area in various houses, and because of the threat that releasing their addresses could cause these people, we have not been able to work on any visits yet.

Earlier this month, one of my bookkeeping clients sponsored a team for the annual Bowlathon fund-raiser for the McLeod County Alliance for Victims of Domestic Violence. One of the key staff people that work at the Alliance is a friend and fellow Minnesota Wisconsin Collie Rescue owner. She and I talked about possibly hosting a visit in the summer at one of the many City parks where the moms and their kids could come and visit with their dogs. Or maybe a local church would let us use one of their rooms to facilitate a visit. I am really stoked on setting up a visit for these families. Many of these kids had to leave their pets behind and are sorely missing their beloved pets. Having a place where they could pet a therapy dog, romp with the dogs, and just allow themselves to laugh and have fun without all the drama that has come into their lives could make such a difference in their lives—and in my own life too. There is nothing better than seeing a child reach out to pet a therapy dog and, once burying their fingers in the fur, seeing a huge smile come across their face. Before my therapy dog career is over, this is definitely on my bucket list.

Facilities for at-risk youth—our group has made several visits to a boys' ranch for at-risk youth. Some of these visits were very heartwarming, and some were complete busts. It all depends which kids are at the facility at the time we visit. Often the older kids are not very interested in seeing the dogs. Some of these poor kids are so jaded from the events that have occurred in their lives while others don't want to let down their guard to show affection for a dog. Some of the best visits we've made were for the younger kids in the facility. One younger boy really bonded with Diane and her dog, Rudy, because Rudy reminded him of his dog at home. Diane spent the whole visit talking to him and she got him to smile and laugh the whole second half of the visit. The next time we visited he had gone home. I certainly hope he has reunited with his beloved dog and is able to get his life back on track.

Demonstrations at the county and state fair—okay, I admit it. I like to entertain people. I sing in a band and I love entertaining people and because of that love of entertaining, I started to think of ways we could entertain people with our therapy dogs. And thus, square dancing with our dogs was born for our chapter. I researched several dog square-dancing groups online and found several square dances that we could do. There really is no dancing involved; instead, it's all about obedience maneuvers with the dogs.

Another fun way to "entertain" people is to do a drill exhibition. When I had my Peruvian Paso horses, I used to ride drill every year with our group. We rode to music and performed various maneuvers such as crossovers or riding in a full barrida, which meant we rode stirrup to stirrup with the other riders and went around the ring. The same kind of maneuvers can be done using our dogs and obedience commands. Do a search on YouTube for the golden retriever drill team. It's great fun and people are fascinated by either square dancing with the dogs or performing drill team events.

Special events—one of the best therapy visits I have made in my career was for the Arts Inspire Day. This event is put on by the McLeod County Social Services department. The head of the department has done a lot of studying and found that children who come from abusive, homeless, and difficult homelives can really be helped by bringing music, movement, art, exercise along with repetitive motions such as petting a dog into their lives. This year was my first visit to this event, and we really didn't know what to expect.

There were approximately fifty kids who participated in the event, which was held at the McLeod County Fairgrounds. We had six pet therapy teams from our group participate. The therapy dogs were posted in one of the fair buildings. The kids came to our building in groups of fifteen or sixteen, and we had them seated in a semicircle. Each team member introduced themselves and their dog, talked about their dog, asked for questions, and then took the therapy dogs around for each of the children to pet.

The kids were fascinated with the fact that both Olaf and Skylar are deaf and yet were doing therapy work. They asked me questions about how I trained them. The best part of the day for me was that several of them wanted me to teach them how I signal for Olaf and Skylar to sit and then they tried it themselves. They were elated when Olaf and Skylar sat.

We saw three groups of about fifteen to sixteen children that day, and each group was wonderful. The kids were respectful and well-behaved. They asked great questions and loved petting all the dogs. At the end of their visit with the therapy dogs, Social Services had purchased cloth dogs for each of the participants to take home. They could color them if they wanted to, but the majority asked each of the therapy dog teams to sign their cloth dog and put their dog's names on the cloth dog. All in all, this was a very gratifying visit.

According to the person who set up this great event for the kids, by far the favorite part of the kids' day was the therapy dogs. How can you have a bad day when you know your precious dogs have impacted kids in such a positive way?

Another special event I attended with the Dynamic Deaf Duo was a visit to Camp Courage. This beautiful facility is located on a lake in central Minnesota and has cabins and meeting rooms for rent. The setting is idyllic and is truly a retreat for those who attend.

A TDI chapter out of the Twin Cities area set up a visit for any TDI therapy team to attend a visit to Camp Courage on a beautiful day in September. The cabins had been rented out for those people suffering with MS. You couldn't ask for better weather as Skylar, Olaf, and I headed out on our new adventure.

Eight teams in total made the visit to Camp Courage that day. It will remain one of my most favorite visits as every one of the participants in the retreat loved petting all the dogs and getting some therapy from them. They all asked great questions about each of the dogs, and many of them were fascinated that Sky and Olaf are deaf yet are still so willing to visit with people they don't know and obviously can't hear. I tell people that dogs don't judge people by what we say—they aren't verbal animals. They access humans by observing body language, and I swear they are able to look into our hearts and determine if we mean them harm or will love them.

At the Camp Courage visit, I talked with one of the therapy teams and found out he had graduated from the same high school as I had but a few years earlier. It was fun reminiscing about all the local hangouts popular at the time. All in all, this visit was one for the memory book, and I'm looking forward to visiting again next year!

Ringing bells for the Salvation Army—another fun visit I made with the therapy dogs this year was to help ring bells for the Salvation Army outside our local Walmart. We were scheduled to help out on two different nights; however, the first night we were supposed to help had temperatures in the single digits with wind chills in the fifteen below zero range. While I love to make therapy visits, standing outside for two hours in that kind of cold just wasn't going to work for me.

The second night we were scheduled was much milder. Skylar and I (Olaf was home nursing a leg injury) along with two other teams from our therapy dog chapter stood outside Walmart to ring bells. We had a great time, took in lots of donations for a very worthy charity, and brought a lot of smiles to weary Christmas shoppers. All three of the teams had such a good time doing this that we decided that we would definitely volunteer again next year!

The possibilities are endless when it comes to visiting people with your therapy dog. I have taken my therapy dogs into one of my bookkeeping clients' store. The workers all love to take a few minutes away from their jobs just to pet the dogs and comment on how soft they are. Open your mind, and think outside the box for places where your dog can brighten up someone's day.

CHAPTER SEVENTEEN

Find Your Purpose

So that's my life story in a nutshell—well, at least as far as how every dog that has come into my life has pointed me in the direction to finding my life's purpose. I am so grateful for all my four-legged furry pals and the unconditional love and affection they have given me throughout my whole life. Whenever I have felt down or depressed, without fail, one of these fur angels will try to snuggle close or lay their head on my body to give me comfort and companionship. I can't begin to express how much I love these creatures as I know they have truly been sent from God to make our lives better. Any abuse of these animals causes me to feel unbelievable outrage and animosity toward the human race.

I joined the Minnesota Wisconsin Collie Rescue (MWCR) and the Minnesota Sheltie Rescue in 2010. I have fostered quite a few collies over the past six years and helped both rescues in transporting rescue dogs to their foster homes and have participated in quite a few fund-raising events for both rescues. I love helping both rescues find permanent "furever" homes for the foster dogs in their care. There is so much good that these organizations do to match up foster dogs with families seeking a four-legged companion. I know I will be involved in both rescues for the rest of my life, hoping that I can help other families find their best friend and companion.

Many have asked me if I have given up on humans in favor of dogs. Well, for the first three years after I got divorced, I did the online dating thing. In fact, I felt that I had to have a man in my life in order to survive. I met many men, some nice, some not so nice. Some of my friends had set me up with various guys, and for a couple of years I had fun dating them. One of them, Bob, is a great guy and became my first bookkeeping client. But he didn't appreciate my dogs living in the house. He felt that dogs should be outdoors in a kennel or at least in the garage. Our dating relationship ended as we both realized that we weren't even close to being on the same page regarding the dogs.

It got more and more difficult to continue online dating. The rejection on both sides was more than I could deal with, so I chose to withdraw from dating. As the years have passed since my divorce, I find that I have grown very comfortable being alone and by myself. My social life is full with making therapy visits, bringing the dogs to events to help out both the Minnesota Wisconsin Collie Rescue and the MN Sheltie Rescue, singing with my acoustic singing group, Stoney Point, and enjoying getting together with my friends.

It took almost sixty-two years for me to feel comfortable in my own skin, to gain back my self-respect, and to finally figure out what my life's purpose is. Since getting divorced, I have found that I want to volunteer for various groups and organizations. Teaching line dance to seniors, acting as treasurer for the historic group in town, running the Adaptive Recreation program for the city, singing in a local community choir, volunteering to transport and foster collies and shelties for both the MN Sheltie Rescue and Minnesota Wisconsin Collie Rescue are ways I have found to give back to other people and the dogs that I love.

I believe it is for each of us to determine why we are here on this earth at this particular time. I surely hope that most people are not like me and have a better sense of self-worth and purpose in life. But for those of you who don't, try to figure out what your joy is in life. What do you love doing? What are you good at? Once you've determined that, see if you can find a way to use that talent to help other people. Are you gifted musically? Make visits to nursing homes and entertain the residents with your musical abilities. Are you a dancer? Put on a dance performance as a benefit for someone having medical issues in your community.

I have always loved singing and have sung in church choirs since I was five years old. Our church got a new minister of music when I was nine years old. He was a good-looking guy whom all of us, from preteens to women in their thirties, found very attractive. I loved singing in his choirs as he had a way to make the music fun.

When I turned eleven, the choir director had tryouts for a new singing group he was forming at church. This group was to be called the Gregorian Singers. The group was scheduled to perform at certain church services and for special events. I was so eager to try out although I was very nervous too. I sang to the best of my abilities at the tryouts, and I anxiously awaited the news of whether I would get picked to sing in this group. The choir director picked fifteen children to be members of this choir. I was so nervous when I got my critique in the mail from him. I remember the written words to this day: "You would be number sixteen. Your voice sounds like Judy Collins." I can't even begin to express how disappointed I was. While I still sang in his group church choirs, I never felt that I had a good voice since obviously I wasn't picked for the Gregorian Singers. I never sang in either junior or senior high school choirs either because I felt I wasn't good enough.

I joined a community choir while living in Kingman. For our spring concert in 2006, an older gentleman who was a former vaudeville actor and I decided to do a duet of the song "Side by Side." We had so much fun singing it together and got so many accolades from people in the audience that singing self-confidence came back to me, and from that performance I realized that I love performing and singing for people. When I moved back to Minnesota, I joined the local community choir and met my future bandmates in that community choir.

About ten years ago, I found out the true reason my former choir director had picked the kids he did for the Gregorian Singers back so many years before. The church senior (adult) choir was having some problems with membership. The number of participants had been dwindling, and he wanted to put a stop to that. He had both a degree in music and in psychology, and he reasoned that he could get some of the senior choir members back if he chose their kids to be in the Gregorian Singers. If the kids were active, it stood to reason that the parents would be active in the music program. And it worked—well, for about two and a half years. Since my parents were not members of the senior choir at that time, I was not even considered for the group. Now I'm not saying that I have a better singing voice than the kids he chose for the group, and I'm not saying that they were better than me. That's a subjective opinion. But I do know that his decision affected my life from age eleven until I turned fifty years old and found out the truth about it.

You're probably wondering why I'm telling you this whole tale. Here's the deal: Don't let anyone deter you from going for your dreams. If you feel your purpose is to sing and bring music into people's lives, listen to the song in your heart, and don't listen to naysayers and negative people. Hold that dream in your mind's eye. Envision yourself singing and entertaining people, and don't let anyone tell you that you can't achieve your dreams.

Each one of us can give back and contribute to the betterment of humankind every day. Random acts of kindness, holding a door for an elderly person, paying it forward and buying the person's groceries behind you in line at the grocery store, or something as simple as just smiling at the people you meet every day—all these little kindnesses can snowball into a huge positive shift in love on the earth.

Well, that's my life's story, and I'm sticking to it. I have made many bad decisions in my life, and I have not lived by the golden rule or the Ten Commandments either. But I am willing to acknowledge all the mistakes in my life and take responsibility for my decisions and actions. I can only go forward in the hopes of living a better, more honest life, and by doing so I hope I can redeem myself. And that's where my wonderful four-legged fur kids come in.

I believe that every dog in my life has been sent to me for a purpose—every one of them! Each dog gave me and still is giving me unconditional love. They have been with me through the lowest times in my life, always steady, always willing to snuggle and give kisses, and always by my side with no questions asked. I know that Mario was sent to me when he was. The summer of 2006 was one of the worst summers of my life. I was distraught over my marriage, the end of my affair, living with an addicted spouse and working a job five days a week that presented me only with the worst that humanity has to offer. I didn't rescue Mario—he rescued me.

Likewise, all three of my deaf shelties I know were sent to me by God. All three needed to be in a home where they are loved and cared for. But more than that, they each have so much love to give to people, and by training them in therapy work, they are probably fulfilling their own purpose according to God's plan.

Until a few years ago, I was so judgmental of people. When I would look at an overweight person, I would immediately start questioning "Why do you look like that?" If someone looked different, I was first up at judging them as being weird or different. Since doing therapy work with my dogs and having three "disabled" dogs, I now view humans with a much kinder eye. I no longer look at people who are "different" in my eyes as being weird but rather that they are expressing their individualism. I never would have come to feelings like that without the aid of my beloved dogs.

And I have finally learned how to live in abundance. I may not have millions of dollars, but I have everything that I need. And my needs are not overwhelming—food, clothing, a home for my dogs and me to live in, satisfying work, activities with my dogs, and a sense of direction when it comes to fulfilling my life's purpose. Yes, I am one lucky human, and I thank God every day for each and every person in my life, for the fact that I do have food, clothing, and a roof over my head and most of all for these blessed fur kids, who have brought so much joy into my life. I am one lucky individual. I didn't live a very honest life in my younger years, and I certainly am not wearing a halo, but I made it through and came out on the other side into the sunshine. I can finally hold my head high as I continue on the path of my life and continue my soul's growth and learn how to best help my fellow human beings. It's been a wonderful life so far!

ABOUT THE AUTHOR

Harley and I

Robin has been an avid dog lover since the age of three, when her family got their first sheltie. Her work life has been as a bookkeeper for large corporations, small businesses, the government, and even her own bookkeeping business. But making therapy visits with her dogs as a volunteer is the most satisfying "job" she has found. In her spare time, Robin loves making therapy visits with her deaf shelties, taking her dogs to various rescue fundraising events, and spending time with friends, family, and her "six-pack" of dogs.

Robin is available for consultations regarding deaf and fearful dog training, dog training questions in general, and to help answer questions about therapy dogs and therapy dog instinct tests. She is also available to help you find your own life's purpose. You can send her a message through her blog page www.weblogdogs.com or on her Facebook page www.facebook.com/redemptionhas4paws/.

CPSIA information can be obtained
at www.ICGtesting.com
Printed in the USA
FFHW01n0326270718
47533097-50943FF